The Thin Places

The Thin Places

A Celtic Landscape from Ireland to the Driftless

KEVIN KOCH

RESOURCE *Publications* · Eugene, Oregon

THE THIN PLACES
A Celtic Landscape from Ireland to the Driftless

Resource Publications
An Imprint of Wipf and Stock Publishers
199 W. 8th Ave., Suite 3
Eugene, OR 97401

www.wipfandstock.com

PAPERBACK ISBN: 978-1-5326-3982-1
HARDCOVER ISBN: 978-1-5326-3983-8
EBOOK ISBN: 978-1-5326-3984-5

Manufactured in the U.S.A.   10/03/18

For my parents, Frank and Ermina Koch,
who rooted me in the Driftless Land but gave me a Celtic name.

And for Marlene and Sharon,
who have charted the course to Tír na nÓg

The silence of the landscape conceals vast presence . . . The earth is full of soul.

—JOHN O'DONOHUE, ANAM CARA

Contents

Acknowledgements

THE THIN PLACES: *A Celtic Landscape from Ireland to the Driftless* has brought together several important threads of my life, from my love of my own home landscape in the bluffs above the Upper Mississippi River to my adopted landscape of Ireland, both of which are mere corners of the sacred earth.

But none of the above developed without the help and guidance of many people.

My wife Dianne is an amazing woman, as my life's loving partner and as a scholar. She was my first reader/responder as these chapters developed and a copy-editor later on. Dianne was also gracious in sending me forth to live in Ireland not once, but twice—for four months in 2012 and two months in 2016. I'm sorry I forgot to tell her that the snow blower has an electric-start cable.

Loras College has been unwavering in its support for this project. President Jim Collins and Provost Cheryl Jacobsen approved my appointment as Ireland Study Abroad Director in Spring 2012, and they along with an anonymous alumni donor awarded me the John Cardinal O'Connor Chair for Catholic Thought in 2015-2016, which offered me both the time and the finances to travel throughout the American Midwest's Driftless region and Ireland. I'm fairly certain that I am the only recipient of the annual award to have submitted reimbursement expenses for guided mountain hikes.

Many other colleagues and friends deserve my thanks. Dana Livingston taught me how to see the prairie, when all I previously appreciated was the woods. My English Department colleague Andy Auge encouraged me to connect my interest in the Driftless Land with Irish Celtic studies, and has been generous with advice and support ever since. My students' enthusiasm for their own nature-based writings kept me refreshed.

A special thank you to my daughter, Angie Koch, who designed the Ireland and Driftless Region maps that adorn the following pages.

In Ireland, the faculty and staff at the Dun Loaghaire Institute of Art, Design, and Technology (IADT), our partner school for the Loras-Ireland study abroad program—have been helpful and supportive as well. I particularly wish to thank the ever-gracious Professor Michael Murphy, who made me feel at home upon first setting foot on Irish soil. I also wish to remember Professor Barry McIntyre, a hill-walking partner and friend who passed away during the writing of this work.

Finally, a thank you to all of the people I interviewed and bothered for follow-up responses here in the Driftless and in Ireland. You have become a wide network of friends to me.

No doubt I have overlooked others whom I should have thanked.

Sacred landscapes are connected hill by hill and valley by valley, even across the oceans. The support of friends and family is no different.

Ireland

Children of Lir

Queen Medb's Grave

MAYO

Achill Island

Westport

Croagh Patrick

Doo Lough

Newgrange

Dublin

Glendalough

Aran Islands

River Shannon

The Driftless Region

WISCONSIN

MINNESOTA

Trempealeau Mounds

Massacre site,
Black Hawk War

Kickapoo Valley
Reserve

Effigy Mounds

Yellow River Forest

Aldo Leopold
Center

Julien Dubuque's Grave • Sinsinawa Mound

The Mines
of Spain

IOWA

Mississippi
River

ILLINOIS

Introduction

Through the Portal

I HAVE BEEN COMING to this perch above the Mississippi River at my home in Dubuque, Iowa, to greet the sunrise eight times a year: the equinoxes, solstices, and the four Celtic feasts midway between each of them. Today is the spring equinox, and an orange glow is blotting through the purple above the eastern bluffs. The sun will be rising in ten minutes, giving me time to sip my coffee and listen for the return of spring birds.

When the sun crowns and burgeons and lets loose from the horizon, it will be a portal that I step through to a Celtic past and a spiritual present, linking places and people and time. Through and back and through again, whichever side I land on when the sun turns yellow-white is where I'll stay till the next passing.

Ireland or the Driftless Land of the Upper Mississippi Valley.

§ § §

Several years ago, I led eleven Loras College students from Dubuque on a study abroad semester in Dublin, Ireland. My students took two courses from Irish professors and two courses from me, one of which was called "The Nature of Nature in Ireland," exploring how people encountered the natural environment throughout Irish history and prehistory.

I had cut my teeth in such studies of my own landscape. A native of Dubuque, Iowa, my personal and writing interests lay in the Driftless Area of the Upper Mississippi Valley, a rugged 20,000 square mile region of northeast Iowa, southeast Minnesota, northwest Illinois, and southwest and central Wisconsin that the glaciers repeatedly bypassed. As such, it is a land of river bluffs and rock towers, steep hills and twisting valleys in the midst of the glacially flattened Midwest. It, too, has a deep, rich story of human interaction with the natural environment.

As the semester abroad came to an end, my students and I gathered one last time in our Dublin classroom. Look, I said, you've been studying the history and landscape of Ireland for four months. But next week we will be back home again. What will this semester abroad mean in the long run? What will you bring home? A bit of Ireland, no doubt. But bring back new eyes for your home. Where you live has a history, too. Like Ireland, your bedrock was formed under ancient seas. Glaciers pummeled it or swept around it, leaving it flat or bluff-ridden. Native Americans arrived about the same time that Paleolithic tribes arrived in Ireland as the glaciers retreated. Modern tribes flourished on the land and then were massacred and displaced by Euro-American invaders, much like the Irish endured centuries of English occupation. Pioneers tore and tamed the land with the plow, and merchants built cities along the rivers and where the trains passed through.

Your home landscape has beautiful scars to trace, just like Ireland's. There are sacred lands with stories asleep in the woods and in the rocks.

And thus this project was born. Having encouraged my students to bring back new eyes for their home landscape, I endeavored to do so myself.

Coming home, I brought new eyes for the *loca sacra*, the sacred local.

§ § §

My sunrise perch is at the Julien Dubuque Monument, the gravesite of the French-Canadian who arrived at these steep limestone bluffs and valleys along the upper Mississippi in 1788 to mine lead alongside the Meskwaki tribe. Two decades after his death in 1810 and immediately after the 1832 displacement of the Meskwaki, immigrant Irish lead miners followed in turn. They and immigrant German shop keepers soon established a river town and named it Dubuque.

Julien Dubuque's grave is marked by a castle-turreted limestone monument, a thirty-foot chess rook sitting on a bluff above the mouth of Catfish Creek, site of the old Meskwaki village. East and south of the Iowa bluff lie the Mississippi River floodplains of northwest Illinois. To the northeast, just barely in view, southwest Wisconsin cliffs drop three hundred feet straight to the river.

The monument is an icon visible from the river, announcing the south entry to this town of 56,000. It also heralds the southern approach to the Driftless Land.

The bluff top monument also warns that here you have left behind clear prairie views and have entered the region of mystery. Steep ravines empty into sinkholes where entire streams disappear into bedrock and erupt back onto the landscape somewhere else. Limestone, shale, and north facing slopes combine to create microclimates, small places with relict plant and animal species linking back to the end of the glacial period. I once tossed a handful of powdery snow across a vertical cave shaft opening and watched the escaping air puff it back like confetti. I had found the hillside where the earth breathes.

I have lived in Dubuque for most of my nearly sixty years. These rock outcrops are my bones, these valleys the creases taking root in my face, these rivers my blood. Body and blood transformed, the land made holy.

This, I have come to understand, is a sacred place.

§ § §

A few years before I started coming to the Julien Dubuque Monument for river bluff sunrises, my wife Dianne and I went hiking just before I was to leave for Ireland as the study abroad director. My wife, a teacher in Dubuque, would be staying behind. In the weeks before my January departure, we took several walks at our favorite Driftless haunts.

Our last such hike was at the Pohlman Prairie just north of Dubuque. The main trail ascends through a hardwood deciduous forest before emerging at a cedar-rimmed prairie on a bluff overlooking the Little Maquoketa River valley. But a less-traveled path halfway up the hillside veers off toward a shelf embankment, and since such paths are more easily followed in winter when the ground is clear of underbrush, we decided to take it. We followed the trail to a small knoll where a heavy mat of mosses and long, flattened grasses draped the stones, protected from winter burn by thick pines, a flash of brilliant green against the winter brown.

"I think we've stumbled into Ireland," I said.

The next day I boarded an Aer Lingus jet with my students and shot through the portal.

§ § §

This is a story about rediscovering place. It is not about wild, exotic, African jungles, the far reaches of Himalayan peaks, or the sweeping expanse of Arctic tundra. It is instead about well-trod landscapes. My own, the Driftless region of the upper Midwest, where ancestors of the Ho-Chunk first

3

hunted megafauna beyond the glacier's edge twelve thousand years ago and where the Mississippi ran red with blood in 1832 when Black Hawk's Sauk tribe was massacred by U.S. troops. And my adopted landscape, Ireland, where human intrigue with the landscape likewise traces back twelve thousand years despite repeated invasions and occupations by Vikings, Anglo-Normans, Tudors, Cromwellians, and the final vestiges of the British Empire.

Unlike wilderness, *place* involves a complex relationship of humans to the land. Abusive relationships, loving, healing. Most of all, remembered, or needing to be remembered. Theologian Philip Sheldrake argues in *Spaces for the Sacred*: "The very word 'landscape' implies an active human shaping rather than a pure habitat . . . There is an interplay between physical geographies and geographies of the mind and spirit."[1]

And sometimes place needs to be looked at afresh. Investigating the Irish landscape has given me new ways to view my own.

How I developed a connection to Ireland is itself a mystery. Not a drop of Irish blood pulses through these Koch arteries. Although my parents gave me a Celtic name, Kevin, I suspect it had more to do with popular names of late 1950s America than with anything Irish. My ancestors were from northern Germany and from Luxembourg. As a kid in Dubuque's German-Irish settler-ethnicity, I was obnoxiously German, as if such a thing mattered anymore. I refused to wear green on St. Patrick's Day or even memorize the date. What country, I smirked as an adolescent, would have as a proverb, "Never bolt your door with a boiled carrot"?

If you are lucky, life will mock your biases. I fell in love with Dianne, my college classmate, whose last name was Noonan, who hailed from Garryowen, Iowa, whose Irish ancestors settled on farms not far from New Melleray Abbey, a Trappist monastery established by Irish monks.

Much of the rest was serendipitous. I took up nature writing, exploring the bluffs and valleys of my home in the Driftless Land and increasingly finding in the mouths of caves and sinkholes the exhaling breath of the spirit of Earth. Loras College had a faculty-led study abroad program in Ireland, and a colleague of mine encouraged me to link the two.

Next thing I knew I was into the portal and emerged onto an Irish landscape.

§ § §

1. Sheldrake, *Spaces for the Sacred*, 15.

"And then there was St. Kevin," wrote the poet Seamus Heaney, retelling the legend of the sixth-century founder of the Irish monastery Glendalough [GLEN-da-lock]. My namesake Kevin, as the story goes, had retired to his hermitage above the monastic city, above the twin mountain lakes that gave Glendalough its name—Valley of the Two Lakes—when he dropped to his knees in prayer with his arms outstretched crucifixion-style. The hut was so small he needed to put one arm out the window, whereupon a blackbird landed in his outstretched hand and laid an egg. Connected now to the web of life, Kevin holds his arm out stiff like a branch for weeks until the eggs are hatched and the young have flown.[2]

And I, another Kevin, fifteen centuries later, stand at the place and feel my feet rooting to the ground, my toes clutching for hold in a sacred soil barely cloaking the bedrock. I am a bit dizzy, having landed and grounded 3,700 miles away from home.

The Irish landscape I found was spiritual, both in the traditional sense of the land of Saints and Scholars but also in the broader way of a landscape steeped in human and geologic story. The immense country bogs, it seemed, retained more than water.

I could also sense the sacred connections of people to landscape dissolving, generationally, before my eyes. But that is a later part of the story.

§ § §

For a small island country roughly the size of Indiana, the Irish landscape is incredibly varied, and as mystical as it is mythical. Mountains and cliff faces rim the coastlines, pummeled and twisted by forces as varied as today's crashing Atlantic waves and the collision of continental plates hundreds of millions of years ago. Moonscapes like the dry, rocky Burren lie literally down the road from rain-swept Connemara. The land can shape-shift: today's turlough [TUR-lock] lake disappears overnight when the water table drops in summer. Mists swallow entire mountains that were in plain view just moments ago. Perhaps the wild and changeable landscape propelled the Irish Celts to view it as sacred, although most indigenous, nature-dwelling cultures have honored their landscapes as sacred as well.

Glaciers shaped much of Ireland, as they did the North American Midwest—although the *absence* of glaciers most significantly defined the Driftless Land. Near Brochagh Mountain in the Wicklow range, my hiking guide points out the rounded mountain tops and U-shaped valleys, both

2. Heaney, Seamus, *Opened Ground, Collected Poems*, 384.

the products of a migrating ice carving the landscape it engulfed. Random granite boulders called erratics were carried across the ice and dropped on the mountaintops when the glaciers retreated. Across the midlands, small s-curved hills called eskers rise above the plains, formed at the base of meltwater streams within the ice. From ancient to near-modern times, these eskers were used as east-west pathways across the midland bogs, being elevated and drier, and offering good vantage points for safety. At the top of Croagh Patrick, Ireland's holy mountain, I gaze out over Clew Bay to find drumlins, formed as the glaciers dragged their trailings into tear-shaped hills. In Clew Bay, the drumlins became islands as the sea level rose again. From the summit of Croagh Patrick they look like hundreds of hump-backed whales taking refuge in port. Perhaps the frequent mists arise from their blowholes.

The most recent glacial period ended twelve thousand years ago, just yesterday in geologic terms. If you count by fifty-year intervals, one per second, 50-100 -150-200, and so on, in one minute you will cover three thousand years. In three minutes and twenty seconds you will be at the glacier's retreating edge.

In North America the last glacial period was called the Wisconsinan, in Ireland the Midlandian. The Midlandian glacier covered nearly all of Ireland, except for a small swath across the south from the mouth of the River Shannon to Waterford. The ice would have been a half-mile thick. All except some of the tallest mountain peaks would have been encased in the slow-flowing mass. Even at Croagh Patrick, which stuck out of the ice pack like a long-abandoned arctic ship mast, the ice-encased lower slopes were rounded into u-shaped valleys.

Archaeologists recently announced a new find that established the earliest evidence of humans in Ireland at 12,500 years ago, beating the previous earliest finds by 2,500 years. The evidence was cut-marks made by human tools to a bear's knee bone, likely made in the butchering of the bear after a kill.[3] These first humans arrived either by boat or by a land bridge that linked Ireland to England to the European mainland while the glacial ice was still retreating. These Paleolithic humans were nomadic hunters and fishermen, leaving no traces of their culture other than spear points and scattered trash heaps of bones and shells.

While the Irish national mythos tells of Celtic culture coming to Ireland by waves of invasion, in reality a gradual osmosis of continental Celtic

3. O'Leary, "Bear Bone Discovery."

culture arrived in the island through trade and cultural interaction around the beginning of the Iron Age (500 BC). A slow and intermingling migration of Celtic peoples from France, Spain, and Britain took place as well. This migration of people and ideas was significant enough that by 200 BC Ireland had developed a Celtic culture and language.

Along with it came Druidic spiritual beliefs tied closely to nature. That said, modernity tends to romanticize Celtic culture. A brief stroll through the National Museum in Dublin to view "bog bodies"—the preserved remains of Celts who had been tossed into the bog after sacrificial, tormented deaths—should serve as a balancing, realistic offset.

Indeed, author Thomas O'Loughlin warns us, "I must sound the warning bell. Notions such as 'the Celtic Church' and 'Celtic spirituality' are common currency at present: there are books, articles, seminars and courses on the subject. In many of these there are confident assertions that 'the Celts believed' or 'the Celts had a different way of looking, or doing, or acting' . . . Such general statements are simply nonsense."[4] Whereupon O'Loughlin leads us headlong into a spirited discussion of Celtic spirituality.

And I follow his lead into the mist.

Water, sacred stones, animals, and oak trees were just a few of nature's key spiritual elements for pre-Christian Celts. Holy wells linked the upper world with the Otherworld as water gushed from unseen places. Such wells were the loci of Ireland's gods and goddesses. The holy well of Tabernault near Sligo was home to a goddess of sovereignty, who demanded from the local king that he be worthy and generous. In turn, the goddess poured forth her waters to ensure good crops and grazing grasses.[5] According to John O'Donohue in his influential book, *Anam Cara*, wells were "threshold places between the deeper, dark, unknown subterranean world and the outer world of light and form. The land of Ireland was understood in ancient times as the body of the goddess. Wells were reverenced as special apertures through which divinity flowed forth."[6]

Bedrock, bone of the earth, was sacred, too. Sacred stones predated Celtic Ireland, with megalithic tombs, stone circles, and stone artwork dating to the Neolithic (ca. 3500 BC) and Bronze Age (ca. 2000 BC) times. The Celts introduced their own holy stones. The Lia Fáil [Foyl] at the Hill of

---

4. O'Loughlin,. *Journeys on the Edges: The Celtic Tradition*, 30.

5. Monaghan, *The Red-Haired Girl from the Bog*, 84.

6. O'Donohue, *Anam Cara*, 86.

Tara, coronation site of the Irish high kings, is a four-foot tall phallus rock upon which the king-elect sat until the rock shouted out his worthiness.

In Celtic animal symbology, birds were protectors and messengers from the gods and goddesses, bees signaled wisdom, cattle symbolized sustenance, horses fertility and sexual vigor. People and animals shape-shifted into each other's forms for advantage or protection, or as the result of punishment or jealousy. King Lir's second wife grows jealous of her step-children's hold on her husband's affections and turns them into swans. Patrick and his followers appear as deer to a local king's men waiting to ambush them.

Trees were of special importance to the Celts, whose Brehons (keepers of the law) developed a hierarchy as to which trees could be cut and which must be left standing. Oak and yew trees ruled the Celtic forest. Poets wrote about sacred oaks associated with local kings. The letters of the Ogham alphabet, the Celts' adaptation of the Roman alphabet, were named for trees.

For reasons to be explored in more detail later, the fifth-century Christian evangelizers of Ireland retained this expression of a sacramental landscape more strongly than did Christian evangelizers on the continent. With the exception, perhaps, of the treatment of the Druid priests themselves, the conversion to Christianity was fairly seamless in Ireland. Holy wells were rededicated to Christian saints associated with the same qualities and powers as their predecessors. Pre-Christian stonework was incorporated into Celtic Christian monasteries. The oak retained its prominence: the name of the city Kildare, for example, simply means the "church [cill] by the oak [dara]."

After the twelfth-century Anglo-Norman invasion, the Irish Church's reverence for nature began to devolve. But an indigenous spirituality persisted alongside the institutional church in Ireland—in pilgrimages, bonfire rituals, worship at holy wells, tying trinkets to prayer trees. All of these practices had their roots in pre-Christianity, and the institutional church gave a nervous, begrudging approval or looked the other way.

Today in an urbanized, modernized, and globalized Ireland, the link of people to place is wearing thin, especially among the younger generations. But the implosion of institutional religion has left an opening for nature spirituality to re-emerge. A revival of Celtic sensibilities infused with strands of Hinduism, Buddhism, and various personal flavorings is helping to re-establish the link of people to landscape.

The spiritual landscape I seek fits any and all of these traditions. Believers may find the tracings of the divine in the flow of a spring-fed creek through a valley. Skeptics and non-believers need only be open to the "something more" of a landscape imbued with memory, even the memory of continental drift and glacial scouring. Spiritual cosmologist Judy Cannato suggests that awe, wonder, and "radical amazement" are the appropriate responses to the wonders of the landscape: "No matter what our religious convictions, it is evident that we live and move and have our being in the midst of a Mystery that is deeper than ourselves and broader than our own creativity and genius can possibly grasp."[7]

§ § §

I could always find in my own Driftless Landscape some of the same intoxicating quirks of landscape iconic to Ireland, though of different kind and scale. Mississippi River bluffs and islands, steep ravines in the woods, limestone tower outcrops, and the archaeological remnants of the Native American and early pioneer past have always fascinated me in my own home.

What was lacking for me was the human story, the kind of deep mythological landscape that links a people to a place through hundreds of generations. This is, of course, a self-inflicted wound of North America. European-Americans—many of whom came from landscapes deeply imbued with a sense of past—committed genocide on the Native American population and forcibly uprooted them from their homelands, and by doing so severed the link between landscape and ancient memory. It is, I believe, partly the reason why we live in a tortured environment.

Native Americans hold on to such stories. For good reason, they hold them closely, as so much else has been taken from them or appropriated.

But a memoried landscape can be resurrected. It begins by knowing the land and knowing our own stories. Then we may go deeper, wherever our mine shafts may lead us.

The earliest Noonans—my wife Dianne's family—arrived in Iowa from County Cork, Ireland, in the mid-1800s and settled in an Irish farming community not far from New Melleray Abbey, itself a clone from Mount Melleray Abbey near Wexford, Ireland. Dianne's Irish ancestors and relatives farmed through the generations, as her brothers still do.

7. Cannato, *Radical Amazement,* 10.

The Koches came to Iowa from northern Germany in the 1880s. Wearied by European wars, they came for peace. Some settled in western Dubuque County farms, but my father's family moved to the town of Dubuque in the early 1900s. He endured the Great Depression there, and as a teenager helped to build the still functioning goldfish pond and limestone rock garden at Eagle Point Park above the Mississippi River as a member of the Civilian Conservation Corps (CCC). Thousands of people still visit the pond every summer.

In farm or city soil, we have set down roots.

§ § §

Let's dispel one myth right from the start. Americans of European descent are fond of saying that their local landscape attracted their ethnic ancestors because it looked like home. The Driftless does not look like Ireland in most regards. Ireland's topography is like a bowl, with mountains and sea cliffs rimming the coastline and glacially flattened lands in the interior. Ireland is rock and bog, sheep and cattle grazing. Ireland's mountains are igneous and metamorphic, formed by magma extrusions or by pressure-heated shape-shifting long ago when the North American continent collided with Europe and rebounded like a bumper car, but left a bit of itself behind in the north of Ireland and Scotland.

The Driftless is river bluff and rock towers, with corn fields and hay fields cultivated between. The Driftless is sedimentary rock—limestone and sandstone and shale—formed on ancient sea floors and uplifted. The Driftless is fossils.

Maybe it wasn't due to a similarity of the landscape, but the Irish did come.

Irish immigrants quickly became the Dubuque area's largest ethnic population in the early 1830s, attracted initially by the lead mines. After the Meskwaki had left the Catfish Creek village but before lands west of the Mississippi were officially opened up to American settlement, a large contingent of miners crossed the river illegally and established a lead mining camp at the Mines of Spain in 1830. The squatters drew up a Miner's Compact, the first set of laws in what would become the state of Iowa. Forty of the fifty-one signers were Irish immigrants.[8]

These first miners were temporarily returned to the Illinois shore by the U.S. military until the Iowa side of the river was open to settlement in

8. Gibson, "Dubuque's Irish History," 38.

1833, after the conclusion of the Black Hawk War. The returned miners named the city "Dubuque" and chartered the city in 1837. By 1860 almost 30 percent of Dubuque households included one Ireland-born parent in a town of 13,000.[9] By the 1870s, a large Irish-immigrant population had settled in the West Hill of Dubuque nicknamed little Dublin, where I live today.

Irish immigration extended out into the county as well. By 1840, there were more Irish farmers than miners in Dubuque County.[10] When Dubuque's first bishop, Matthias Loras, recruited twenty-two Irish Cistercian monks in 1849 to establish a new monastery in western Dubuque County, it sparked further waves of Irish immigration to nearby farming communities (providing context for my wife's family's later immigration).

German-born immigrants exceeded the Irish-born in Dubuque to a slight degree by 1860, setting the stage for my own family's eventual immigration. With some local variation, Irish and German immigration dominated the Driftless region.

§ § §

Four years after returning from teaching abroad in Dublin, I stepped through the portal again, this time alone to confront the landscape one more time and press to feel its breath. With a sabbatical from teaching I tramped through the Wicklow Mountains and wandered among the headstones and ruins of Glendalough. Then I headed west to live in the town of Westport for two months. Located on Clew Bay on the Atlantic coast, Westport appealed to me because it was a small town (easier for me to get to know people), was fairly central on the western coast (easy to travel north and south), and teemed with nearby archaeological and natural wonders. I joined a local hiking and bicycling group. By car, bicycle, and on foot, I tracked down Neolithic and Bronze-Age tombs and celestial markers, stone circles, early Christian grave stones, monastic ruins, and the fading evidence of the Great Famine on the landscape. I imagined the glaciers carving out valleys in the mountains and depositing island-drumlins in Clew Bay. And I talked with townspeople over coffee at Christy's Market and around the town and region about their own visions of a spiritual landscape.

And, of course, I climbed Croagh Patrick, the iconic sharp-peaked mountain located just outside of Westport and a visual landmark for miles

9. Auge., "Immigration Patterns into Dubuque County up to 1860," n.d., n.p.

10. Auge, "Immigration Patterns into Dubuque County up to 1860," n.d., n.p.

around. Already sacred to pre-Christians, Croagh Patrick is said to be the forty-day fasting site of Saint Patrick in the mid-400s, from which legend says he "banished" Ireland's never-present snakes. Croagh Patrick is perhaps Ireland's most-climbed mountain, with up to 15,000 pilgrims ascending it on Reek Sunday (the last Sunday in July). On just about any other weekend of the year the mountain still groans under the feet of innumerable climbers. And it is not an easy climb, for all of its foot-traffic. Loose stones and a sharp final ascent make the path a challenging climb and an even more perilous descent.

At the foot of Croagh Patrick rests one of Ireland's most iconic memorials to the Famine, a 1997 sculptured coffin ship whose rigging is ligamented with bronze skeletons. I visited the monument in the pre-dawn dark of Easter Sunday. Floodlights seemed to have detached the ship from its moorings, and it hung in suspension above the earth, waiting to float or fly away in the impending storm.

Can stories be carried away in boats?

SPIRITUAL LANDSCAPES

In what way, then, do the facts of geology, paleontology, archaeology, and history—migrations of rocks, ice, and people—bring together Ireland and Driftless Land of the American Midwest?

For me the connection lies in seeing my home with new eyes made more aware of a spiritual landscape. Noel Dermot O'Donoghue, scholar of early Celtic Christianity, describes the act of seeing the "mountain behind the mountain," of perceiving an "imaginal" world that sees beyond the observable and literal to a "sphere of living presences, at once physical and spiritual."[11] To perceive such a world brings it to life again, awakens it, coaxes it from the Thin Places, i.e., those places of Celtic lore where the veil between this world and the Otherworld is thin and permeable. In a modern context, the Thin Places are those locales that shimmer with the mystical presence of the storied past.

And so, on the flanks of Croagh Patrick on the west coast of Ireland, perceiving the mountain behind the literal mountain, I awaken the pressurized heat of colliding continents half-melting and warping the bedrock. The weight and grinding of glacial ice slowly scours out the valleys in my mind's

---

11. O'Donoghue, *The Mountain Behind the Mountain*, 22.

eye. I walk in the still-present footpaths of Neolithic peoples and St. Patrick and throngs of medieval pilgrims.

At the Julien Dubuque Monument, three hundred feet above the Mississippi River, I bring back the glacial meltwater roiling down from the north, hauling ice floes and scouring the valley. I imagine the elders or a visitor from another tribe, twelve thousand years ago, telling stories of the mile-high ice cliffs not so very far away, of the thunderous roar they make as they calve on warm summer days. Irish immigrant lead miners up in the bluffs south of me, just beyond the old Meskwaki settlement, find life again, as do the German shop keepers and factory owners starting new lives in the fledgling town behind me.

I am alone on this Mississippi River bluff in the Driftless Land, but it is crowded with the past.

§ § §

As I began to think of the long presence of human story on the Irish landscape in relation to my landscape in the Driftless, several principles of a Celtic and Celtic-Christian spirituality of place took shape. These principles are not exhaustive of Celtic culture, nor are they exclusive to Celtic culture, but in this combination they suggest a Celtic manner of seeing. These became my new lens for viewing my own landscape: *The land is sacred; The Creation is good; The Holy transforms the familiar; Time is cyclical and elastic in the Thin Places; Animals shape the human world; The Holy inhabits the austere, remote places; Story gathers in the landscape; Poets give voice to the landscape.*

I needed to see my home afresh on its own terms. I revisited old haunts in the Driftless and found new ones as well. I would have to learn the traditions and stories of my ancestors from these hills and—perhaps more importantly—learn the stories of the indigenous peoples who lived here before them.

On certain symbolic days—four Celtic feasts in the Wheel of the Year and four annual celestial events—I would trek to my bluff above the Mississippi River to greet the sunrise:

- December 21: The Winter Solstice, the day of shortest sunlight;

- February 1, Imbolc [EE-molc], the feast of the birthing of lambs;

- March 21, Spring Equinox, day of equal light and dark;

- May 1, Bealtaine [Be-AHL-tin-eh], the extinguishing and relighting of hearth fires;

- June 21, Summer Solstice, the day of longest sunlight;

- August 1, Lughnasa [Lune-AH-sah], the feast of light and early harvest;

- September 21, Fall Equinox, day of equal light and dark;

- and October 31, Samhain [SAH-win], the beginning of the Celtic year when the thin veil between the living and spirit worlds dissolves in the mystical locations called Thin Places.

On these Celtic feasts and astronomically significant days I foster the connection between my home landscape and my adopted one.

Coming home, I bring new eyes for the *loca sacra*.

§ § §

Today is the spring equinox back in the Driftless. The glow above the Illinois bluff has intensified, and an orange ball is crowning at the horizon. The sun is rising not far from Sinsinawa [sin-sin-AH-wah] Mound, a swell on the horizon visible for twenty, thirty miles in every direction. I stare and ease its lift till it is full and round and orange above the bluff. The orange leaks and spreads like a broken yolk. At river level, three hundred feet below the bluff, a mist noses out the reaches of the valley. Nine-Mile Island, just visible before dawn from my bluff-top view, rises out of the thin fog.

And then I step into the portal and am gone again.

(Photography corresponding to respective chapters of The Thin Places *can be found at http://www.kevinkochdriftlessland.net.)*

Chapter 1

Winter Solstice: The Land is Sacred

THE WINTER SOLSTICE

SIX INCHES OF SNOW have fallen overnight before the winter solstice. I've set the alarm for 5:30 a.m., allowing extra time to get to Julien Dubuque's grave for the sunrise. The snowplow hasn't cleared the busy street in front of my house, so it surely hasn't plowed a path to the monument.

I don't trust my car's traction on the hills en route to the blufftop monument, so I have two choices: go back to bed or leave now and snowshoe to the grave.

Of course I choose the latter.

In the pitch dark I drive down to the end of the long and level avenue where I live and stop at the trailhead that leads to the grave. A hint of dawn has just awakened in the eastern sky as I strap on my snowshoes and disappear down the path.

Just enough dawn glow pokes through a break in the tree canopy to guide me along the trail. The trees on either side form a solid dark wall, while the patch of sky above slowly brightens during the twenty-minute trek.

By the time I reach the blufftop, it is light enough to see the monument and across the river valley. The clouds are thick, though—there will be no blazing sunrise this morning. I stand for a while at the monument and gaze silently across the ice-encrusted river to the maze of frozen backwaters amid the winter-browned floodplain forest on the Illinois shore.

The world around me looks unreal, or real in unworldly ways. The fresh snowfall is rich and creamy and untouched. It is as quiet as a hermitage. My breathing confirms there is spirit here, mine and that of the ages.

The winter solstice—December 21 in the northern hemisphere—is known as the "shortest day of the year," meaning that the number of daylight hours is at its nadir and will now slowly increase.

It is both the bleakest day of the year and the day of great hope.

§ § §

Throughout the northern latitudes, ancient peoples celebrated the winter solstice. It was in part a practical matter. Marking the shortest day of the year reasonably predicts when it will be time to plant again. But it is a spiritual event as well: gods and goddesses return from the underworld, the landscape reawakens. Passionist monk and cosmologist Thomas Berry explains, "In most religious traditions, diurnal moments of transformation, dawn and dusk, the mysterious transition from day to night and from night to day, are profoundly religious moments to be observed with appropriate prayer and ritual," and the dawn of the winter solstice is the greatest among these. [1]

These transitional, liminal points in the wheel of the year were particularly powerful in the Thin Places.

NEWGRANGE

If light were liquid, it would steal in like this, a golden wash creeping up the passageway at dawn, illuminating the center of the tomb.

This was a simulation, the guide at Ireland's Newgrange told us, carefully re-enacted with light bulbs on dimmer switches. But on the Winter Solstice, a lucky twenty lottery winners could view the real thing, just as ancient priests and clan leaders must have done 5,000 years ago. On the shortest day of the year, at dawn, the sun clears the horizon and spills into the passageway, lighting the tomb's interior that is dark the rest of the year, and proclaiming to all of Ireland that spring will come again.

Newgrange is a supreme example of an Irish Neolithic (Stone Age) passage tomb and astronomical temple, built a thousand years before the pyramids and Stonehenge. Located thirty miles northwest of Dublin atop

---

1. Berry, *The Christian Future and the Fate of the Earth*, 57.

one of the tallest hills near the River Boyne, the massive circular tomb stretches nearly three hundred feet in diameter and rises nearly forty-five feet above its natural mound.

Ninety-seven glacial boulders, a ton or more in weight, ring the base of the structure, decorated with haunting chiseled spirals. Two hundred thousand tons of small stones complete the mound, traceable to ancient quarries up to twelve miles away. The exposed face of the tomb is decorated with small quartz stones, giving the appearance of white-wash.

When the guide called for us, we ducked beneath a weathered stone slab and entered the tomb. We hustled, bent-backed, along a narrow passageway leading sixty feet inward from the eastern face of the tomb and slightly uphill to the center. At its center, the passageway terminates with three small chambers for the dead, perhaps for cremains. The center opens to a tall ceiling of 450 stone slabs spiraling upward to a domed top.

A separate opening called the roofbox allows the sunrise to wash the central chambers for about seventeen minutes on the Winter Solstice and a few days on either side. Though the ancient rituals are lost to time, archaeologists speculate that the ashes of the year's deceased may have been brought into the three chambers to await the coming of the Winter Solstice light.

Perhaps the souls of the dead followed the retreating light back out of the tomb like an ebbing tide.

The alignment of Newgrange with the winter solstice isn't accidental. Neolithic Irish knew the land they lived in, knew the stars and skies. Another nearby mound, called Knowth, aligns with the Autumn equinox sunrise. The Winter Solstice sunset floods the interior of Slieve Gullion in Northern Ireland seven hours after Newgrange has been washed with sunrise.

Ireland is dotted with 229 known Neolithic passage tombs, many of which doubled as astronomical temples. Forty of these are found near Newgrange in an area called Bru na Boinne, an ancient fertile farming community where people settled long enough to construct the massive structures over generations and centuries.

Then time washed over Bru na Boinne. The tombs and astronomical temples were forgotten. The massive structures held, but soil and grasses overtook the cairns and slumped over their sides. Newgrange became a hillside swell, grazed by sheep and cattle. But some memory must have settled over it because the local people knew it as a fairy hill, not to be disturbed. Fairy hills in Ireland were those places where long-forgotten but curious human constructions or other oddities of the landscape were considered to be the home places of the fairies (aka the sidhe [she] or the Tuatha De Danann), a half-divine race defeated by the arriving Celts of ancient mythology. The fairies were consigned to the underworld, but occasionally crossed over into this world in the Thin Places. To disturb a fairy hill invited their mischief.

The conquering British held no such taboos. In 1625, an English landowner attempted to quarry the site. Luckily, the first digs sunk down into the passage doorway, and centuries of stony sleep were reawakened. The quarry venture was abandoned, but the entry remained partially open. The following centuries saw occasional daring tourists. Graffiti inside the tomb confirms visitors from the 1800s.

Professor Michael O'Kelly of the Archaeology Department at University College-Cork began excavating and restoring the tomb from 1962 to 1975. The interior passage had remained intact over the centuries, buried beneath the slumping cairn, but the entryway and roof box, as well as the exterior walls and decorated stones, had to be unearthed.

O'Kelly had heard rumors that on a certain day of the year the sunrise would light up the stonework outside the tomb. What then of the interior? Noting the southeast alignment of the entryway, O'Kelly surmised that if there were anything at all to the rumor, then it must refer to sunrise on the Winter Solstice. On December 21, 1967, O'Kelly quietly slipped inside, alone, minutes before dawn, half fearful that the sun god Dagda, purported by mythological tradition to have built the tomb, would bring it down on top of him.

Then the golden glow crept in, "lighting up everything as it came," said O'Kelly:

> The light began as a thin pencil and widened to a band of about 6 in. There was so much light reflected from the floor that I could walk around inside without a lamp and avoid bumping off the stones. It was so bright I could see the roof 20 feet above me. I expected to hear a voice, or perhaps feel a cold hand resting on my shoulder, but there was silence. And then, after a few minutes, the shaft of light narrowed as the sun appeared to pass westward across the slit, and total darkness came once more.[2]

2. "Professor Michael J. O'Kelly." Knowth.com.

O'Kelly had become the first person since ancient times to witness the Winter Solstice sunrise inside the tomb.

Since the renovation of the tomb, the Brú Na Bóinne Visitor Centre holds a lottery drawing to select ten persons plus an invited guest to enter the tomb for the 8:58 a.m. sunrise each day for the five days surrounding the solstice. In 2015 alone, over 34,000 people applied for the Newgrange winter solstice lottery.

Dublin's Mary Gibbons[3] was one of the lucky ones to observe the solstice sunrise inside Newgrange in 2015, connecting, she says, to what her Irish ancestors may have experienced over five thousand years ago. A group of twenty participants, including Mary, entered the chamber in total darkness. The chamber lightened gradually with the dawn. Then, says Mary, a "thin line of sun came in, gradually spreading and lighting up the entire chamber. You could see people's faces, but everyone was silent—it was an individual rather than a group experience. Some people took off their jewelry and put it on the floor as if to capture the beam of sunlight."

Mary insists that she is not an emotional person, nor someone who puts much stock in spirituality. "I've always seen Newgrange as an astronomical rather than a spiritual site. But when you get in there and it actually happens, well, I still applauded the engineers, but you begin to see the power of the sun and your connection to it. You realize this is your moment with the sun, individual and personal."

"Coming out, my first reaction was that it is unfortunate that the Church stopped all this worship of the sun. It's such a natural thing to worship."[4]

Our guide slowly dimmed the lights until we stood in darkness so complete we couldn't see our own hands and feet. Next, he slowly brought up another set of lights mimicking the winter solstice sun creeping up the passageway till it lit the center of the tomb. After the prescribed time, our guide led us back outside where the clouded daylight still burned our eyes. But before we left, he said that a sliver of light from outside is visible if you lie on the floor and peer down the passageway.

One of my students lingered a few moments back in the tomb. She stretched herself face-first across the floor of the 5,000-year-old tomb and

3. Mary Gibbons is owner/operator of Mary Gibbons Tours, which offers history-based tours of Newgrange and the Hill of Tara.

4. Gibbons, Telephone Interview.

saw for herself the thin line of sunlight leaking in from the outside world. When she told me this, weeks later, I couldn't have been more proud.

THE LAND IS SACRED

On Easter morning the sky was beginning to lighten over Clew Bay just outside of Westport as I ducked through the tiny stone doorway and entered the ruins of Murrisk Abbey to attend Dawn Mass. The jagged walls of the ruins were silhouetted against a purple sky.

Murrisk Abbey was a short-lived fifteenth-century Augustinian Friary situated at the base of Croagh Patrick. By the end of the sixteenth century, the friars had been driven out by Oliver Cromwell's forces solidifying Protestant British rule. The friary was reduced to ruins.

But on this twenty-first-century Easter dawn, it had come to life again with a hundred or so participants gathered for Mass. Storms were on the horizon, with thunder and lightning reported in nearby Galway. Father Charlie promised that he "would not test the Lord" with a long homily but would move the service along quickly. The sky first lightened a bit with the dawn but then darkened again, and as a pelting rain let loose the abbey sprang a new and colorful roof, with umbrellas plentiful enough to keep the congregation dry.

Outdoor Easter dawn Masses are common in Ireland, especially in the west. The tradition links back to the nature spirituality of pre-Christian times. The Celtic culture that arrived or evolved around 500 BC brought with it, writes Dolores Whelan, founder of the Iomlanú Centre for Healing and Creative Living, the belief that "the spiritual world infuses the material world, and that the material world emerges from the spiritual, non-material world."[5] In the Celtic tradition, the veil between spiritual and material worlds is thin.

Early Celtic Christian Ireland embraced this pre-Christian sense of a sacramental landscape to a degree not replicated elsewhere by the Christian Church. Ireland's physical distance from the Roman Church and Empire afforded the Celtic Christian Church a certain degree of independence.

Christianity was first embraced and promoted by the Roman Empire in 313 AD when Emperor Constantine announced the protection of Christian practice in the Edict of Milan. It is difficult to know, thereafter, which elements of Christian practice were theological and which were culturally

5. Whelan, "Celtic Spirituality: A Holy Embrace of Spirit and Nature," 20.

influenced by the Roman Empire. The Romans, for example, elevated the city over the countryside. The Christian Church in turn, became citified. Bishops resided in cities, and even the word "pagan" originally meant a "country person." A "heathen" was he who lived out on the heath.

The Romans had conquered southern Britain by the first century AD. They must have stood on the western shore and looked across to Ireland—the land they called Hibernia, the Land of Winter—and decided their empire had gone far enough. Ireland, left alone by the Romans and not Christianized until after the Empire's withdrawal from England in 410 AD, never adopted Roman ways. Ireland was an island without cities. Families and small groups of kin built their dwellings and kept their herds within earthen ringforts or raths (circular stone forts), but cities themselves did not appear until the settlement of Vikings in the 900s.

So when Patrick and other early missionaries brought Christianity to Ireland shortly after the Romans left Britain, they came to an intensely rural land. Celtic Christianity embraced these rural sensibilities, and retained or transformed much of the pre-Christian mythos as well. St. Patrick and his entourage shape-shift into a herd of deer like figures from a Celtic tale. St. Brigit channels the goddess Brigit as a patroness of fire and the arts. St. Columbkille (or Colmcille, Dove of the Church) forbids the felling of oak trees, sacred to the preceding Druidic tradition. As a result, the conversion of the Irish to Christianity was fairly seamless.

This Celtic Christian Church was notably different from the Romanized Church, but was not consciously in rebellion—the Reformation was still a millennium away. Still, the lack of cities in Ireland reduced the influence of city-dwelling and uniformity-commanding bishops. Local monastery abbots held more influence than bishops, and the Irish church went on its merry individual way.

At the same time, it is easy to overstate the continuity of nature reverence from pre-Christian to Christian Ireland. Two poems from the respective traditions illustrate a transitioning view of nature and divinity. The pre-Christian mythical settler-poet Amergin [AH-ver-zhin] describes a pantheistic spiritual landscape in which the divine equates directly to nature:

> I am the wind which breathes upon the sea
> I am the ocean wave, . . .
> I am a sunbeam,
> I am the fairest of plants,

> I am a wild boar in valour,
> I am a salmon in the water,
> I am a lake in the plain, . . . [6]

St. Patrick, on the other hand, shifts the Christian spiritual landscape, depicting a God who is at once both present throughout the creation yet transcendent above it:

> Our God is the God of all things,
> the God of heaven and earth,
> the God of the sea and the streams,
> the God of the sun, moon and stars,
> the God of the great high mountains and the deep glens, the God above heaven, in heaven and under heaven. And he has a household — heaven and earth,
> and the sea and all that they contain. [7]

There are two ways to view this Christian shift: either as repudiating the pre-Christian equivalence of God and nature or as presenting the pre-Christian Celtic tradition as the beginning of an arc that completes itself in Christianity.

Continental Roman Christianity tends to the former, says contemporary self-described Celtic monk and priest Dara Molloy.[8] Monotheism itself, he argues—beginning with the Israelites and continuing with Christianity—drove a wedge between believers and the natural world. In polytheistic societies, writes Molloy, "People project their mythology onto the surrounding landscape, so that, in everything they see or encounter, an element of their own beliefs is reflected back to them. Their landscape speaks to them and provides the spiritual container for their lives."[9] For monotheistic believers, Molloy writes, "The land is the creation of one god who lives elsewhere. This god does not dwell in the land nor is he even part

---

6. "The Mystery," *1000 Years of Irish Poetry*, 3.

7. Stokes, ed., *The Tri-Partite Life of Patrick*, 101.

8. Ordained a priest in the Society of Mary (Marist Fathers) in 1977, Dara Molloy has lived as a Celtic monk and priest on Inis Mór, Aran Islands since 1985. In 1996 he announced his departure from the Marist Fathers and Roman Catholicism. Dara and his wife Tess Harper run a Celtic spiritual centre, or aistir, called An Charraig on Inis Mór.

9. Molloy, *The Globalization of God*, 63.

of the cosmos. The creator god relates to the earth the way humans relate to something they have made. He looks on from outside the universe."[10]

Molloy views Celtic Christianity differently from its continental cousin, however, focused more on the arc of spiritual evolution than repudiation of pre-Christian sensibilities. The Celtic Christian Church, he writes, grew "upon the fertile topsoil of an earlier Celtic spirituality . . . Dagda, the great Celtic father god, is a prefiguration of God the Father; Lugh, the Celtic god of light, is a Christ figure who defeats the forces of darkness."[11] In a similar way, Redemptorist priest and author John O'Ríordáin believes that in Celtic Christianity, the Christian God does not so much destroy ancient Celtic sensibilities as brings them to fulfillment.[12]

St. Patrick himself seems to have regarded the natural world with a sacredness that would only be met on the continent by St. Francis of Assisi seven hundred years later. Patrick's "Deer Song" strongly signals a sacramental God who is both present in and transcendent beyond the natural world:

> I arise today
> Through the strength of heaven,
> Light of sun,
> Radiance of moon,
> Splendour of fire,
> Speed of lightning,
> Swiftness of wind,
> Depth of sea,
> Stability of earth,
> Firmness of rocks.[13]

The early Celtic Christian laity likewise viewed the natural world as magical and holy, much like their pre-Christian ancestors. Irish Christians turned out on Easter morning to watch the sun "dancing up and down in exultation at the joyous resurrection."[14] Perhaps such traditions morphed from the pre-Christian, even pre-Celtic, practices such as gathering at the

---

10. Molloy, 62.

11. Molloy, *The Globalization of God*, 180.

12. O'Ríordáin, *The Music of What Happens*, 45-46.

13. Hoagland, ed., *1000 Years of Irish Poetry*, 13.

14. O'Donoghue, *The Mountain Behind the Mountain*, 17.

Neolithic Boheh Stone near Westport, from which vantage point the sun appears to roll down the side of Croagh Patrick twice each year.

Edward Sellner, in *Wisdom of the Celtic Saints*, sums up the continuity of Celtic Christianity from the pre-Christian world:

> This Celtic Christian spirituality was very much the child of the pagan culture which preceded it, one that valued poetic imagination and artistic creativity, kinship relations and the warmth of a hearth, the wonder of stories and the guidance of dreams. It was a spirituality profoundly affected by the beauty of the landscape, the powerful presence of the sea, and the swift passage at night of the full moon across open skies.[15]

Selner further notes that early Irish Christian mystics frequently established their monasteries and oratories on the very sites where druids and priestesses "had once taught and worshipped—in the midst of oak groves or near sacred springs, on the shores of secluded lakes, or on misty islands far out at sea.[16]

The kinship of the Celtic Irish church with the natural world would devolve over the ensuing centuries. The Celtic church finally gave in to Rome on such matters as determining the date for Easter, or how to wear monastic tonsures (Irish monks shaved the front half of their heads instead of the more iconic continental monk's top-shave). Anglo-Norman colonization promoted bishops over abbots and brought continental monastic orders to Ireland. The British colonial anti-Catholic Penal Laws in some ways drove the Irish church back to nature by necessity, forcing clandestine outdoor Masses offered at Mass Rocks. But at the same time, resistance to British religious oppression drove the Irish to a more direct embrace of the Romanized church, including its proclivity toward cityscapes and church buildings over landscapes and the cathedrals of trees. Slowly the Celtic belief in a sacred creation was replaced by the continental church's denigration of the body and the physical world.

The implosion of institutional religion in Ireland has left an opening for modern nature spiritualties to re-emerge. More and more, people engage in spirituality and spiritual acts without the blessing of "outside agencies" like institutional churches, says Molloy. Whether such indigenous and individualized spiritualties invoke ancient practices like visiting holy wells and lighting sacred bonfires or are spiritually reconceived acts like

15. Sellner, *Wisdom of the Celtic Saints*, 16.
16. Sellner, *Wisdom of the Celtic Saints*, 22.

gardening, dancing, or healthy, natural eating, the consequence may well lead to a return to "bioregional spirituality," a "right relationship between the local people and local sources of their food, clothing and shelter."[17]

§ § §

The rain let up as the Easter Dawn Mass at Murrisk Abbey came to end, and we all closed our umbrellas, murmured our thank-you's to Father Charlie, who had served us through the downpour, and ducked down through the tiny doorway to exit the ruins. Clew Bay was at high tide, and several of us paused at the shore to watch small waves gathering in the breeze. To the west, Croagh Patrick loomed, its peak just barely visible in the squall still emptying onto the mountain.

This is an old, old land, I realized, but no older than my own in the Driftless Land. The landscape has its stories. That's what makes it spiritual to believers and nonbelievers alike. The deeper the stories—geological, religious, historical, personal—the more spiritual it is.

But people can lose connection with the land. It may happen through genocide, through which an indigenous people's stories are lost, such as has been the case throughout much of North America. It may happen through modernization, which offers the false impression that we can with impunity trade physical places for virtual ones. Even modern environmentalism can ironically dissociate us from spiritual landscapes if there is no room to consider the earth's stories. Ireland has seen erosion of the connection to nature. As Ireland becomes increasingly urbanized, modernized, and globalized, the link of people to place is wearing thin, especially among the younger generations. The same has been true of North America for quite some time.

Thomas Berry warns us, "As we lose our experience of the songbirds, our experience of the butterflies, the flowers in the fields, the trees and woodlands, the streams that pour over the land and the fish that swim in their waters; as we lose our experience of these things our imagination suffers in proportion, as do our feelings and even our intelligence."[18]

Even so, about a hundred people had gathered in the dark at Murrisk Abbey despite the imminent threat of rain on Easter morning. They could have slept in, gone to church some place with a roof and heat, or ignored the ancient feast altogether. But they chose instead the promise of an Easter

17. Molloy, *The Globalization of God*, th.

18. Berry, *The Christian Future and the Fate of the Earth*, 42.

dawn's raw encounter with the elements under the open skies of an abbey ruins.

I call such moments sacred.

EFFIGY MOUNDS NATIONAL MONUMENT

Albert LeBeau,[19] Cultural Resources Program Manager at Effigy Mounds and member of the Lakota Nation, bounces us up the utility road en route to the Marching Bears. His young assistant, Cultural Resources Interpreter Sheila Oberreuter, sits in the back and playfully needles Albert about the time he got the pickup stuck in the muddy lane last spring. My writer's notebook looks like the printout of a cardiac patient's heartbeat. Or perhaps a seismograph report, since paper and pen on several occasions have taken off in different directions as we've clawed our way up five hundred feet above the river.

Effigy Mounds National Monument preserves and protects over two hundred burial and ceremonial mounds along the Mississippi River in northeast Iowa. Thirty-one of the mounds are shaped as bears or birds in one of the nation's most significant Native American historical and spiritual sites. The national monument was established in 1949 after a failed attempt to create an Upper Mississippi River National Park that would have included the mounds and several nearby environmentally and culturally important properties that became, instead, the Yellow River State Forest (Iowa), Pikes Peak State Park (Iowa), and Wyalusing State Park (Wisconsin). The result is almost seven thousand acres of relatively undisturbed natural river corridor. Much of the region has been designated an Important Bird Area for waterfowl, raptors, and migratory tropical birds who hatch and rear their young along the Upper Mississippi before returning south.

The mounds under the protection of the National Park Service were built by Woodland Period Native Americans from 500 BC to 1200 AD. Conical and linear mounds are among the oldest, while the bird and bear effigies were constructed near the end of the era. The Marching Bear unit features ten bear-shaped mounds arranged roughly head-to-tail in single file formation pointed southward along the Mississippi bluff top. Accompanying the bears are three bird effigies, their wings spread as if in flight and their heads pointed toward the river beneath the bluff. Two of the birds scout out ahead of the marching bears while the third corrals the rearmost

19. LeBeau, Personal Interview.

into line. The largest bear measures 137 feet from nose to tail, and the largest bird's wingspan is 212 feet.

Archaeologist Phil Millhouse[20] suggests that the bear and bird shapes symbolize the underworld and upperworld, respectively, keeping them in balance. The birds that bracket the marching bears maintain a balance as well. But the shapes are also likely associated with the clans that built them. And the act of *building* the mounds—of communities coming back together after a winter apart from each other—is significant too. It is "all one thing," Millhouse explains. "It's like an old cathedral with all of its symbolism, but in this case inscribed across the landscape."[21]

Dr. Clark Mallam, deceased former professor of anthropology at nearby Luther College, argued that the mounds were "metaphorical expressions that stress the idealized state between nature and culture—harmony and balance." The mounds were a means to insure "the continuation of the annual cycle of life, expressed in seasonal regeneration of plants and animals. Perhaps this explains why the effigies appear to be integrated with the earth while they simultaneously emerge from it."[22]

As we reach the top of the bluff and exit the truck, Albert wonders aloud, "What was the landscape telling the mound builders?" Each of the bear effigies, he explains, once contained a "heart stone." This was a stone not native to the region, brought in and placed at the location of the heart in the effigy animal. None of the heart stones remain in place today. What did this heart stone mean, and why was it brought in from somewhere else?

The area in which the effigy birds and bears reside is kept neatly trimmed by the national monument personnel, although the grasses on the mounds themselves are only cut once or twice a year and occasionally burned to trim out woody plants, whose roots can damage the mound shapes. There's a fine line, LeBeau explains, between too little and too much TLC for the mounds. Left alone, the surrounding woods would soon overtake them. Not only would the mounds be hard to see, but the natural cycle of tree and root growth, toppling and decay would eventually disfigure the mounds. But too much intrusion could damage the mounds as well.

20. Phil Millhouse is an archaeologist who grew up in Northwest Illinois, part of the Driftless Region in which he now practices his work. He earned his PhD in Archaeology from University of Illinois at Urbana-Champaign. Millhouse has worked for the Illinois Department of Transportation and for the Illinois State Archaeological Survey, and now runs his own archaeology consulting service called Red Gates Archeology.

21. Millhouse, Personal Interview.

22. Mallam, "Ideology from the Earth: Effigy Mounds in the Midwest," 61.

Constant mowing would not only disfigure the mounds and compress their soils, but would be contrary to the natural settings in which they occur.

Even Native Americans differ on how or whether the mounds should be preserved, says LeBeau. While most are appreciative of the Park Service's work, others believe that nature should be allowed to take its course.

Despite the best of theories, how and why these mounds were constructed remains a matter of conjecture. Located at the confluence of the Mississippi and Wisconsin Rivers, the Effigy Mounds area would have been a gathering place of many clans in spring, summer, and fall before they dispersed in smaller groups again in winter.

When spring brought the clans back together—some of them bringing with them the bones of those who had died over winter—they met and worked and negotiated on holy ground. Part of the mound-building involved interring the dead.

But the mound-builders didn't merely dig up soil from one spot on the bluff and heap it on the mounds. Some of the mound soils were hauled up, basket by basket, from the river shore, in pathways winding up the bluff. Perhaps the river soils added another layer of the sacred to the mounds. Perhaps the rough road our pickup climbed today was one such footpath.

The people who built the effigies, says Albert, "were here for ceremony and then would leave, perhaps living in small villages along the river for the spring, summer, and fall. Effigy Mounds was a place to converge, discuss, and to have ceremonies."

Speculating a bit, Albert muses, "Perhaps these people had an ancient memory of the Driftless Area as a 'refugia' going back to the ice ages. During the glacial period, the Driftless offered food, water, shelter. Through the ages it could have remained a refuge, a gathering place, passed down through generations as a sacred place." Albert pauses and then adds, "It still is a gathering place . . . for birders, leaf watchers, visitors to the Mounds."

The Ho-Chunk of Southwest Wisconsin claim lineage back to the earliest peoples who entered the Driftless, as well as to the mound-builders themselves. This longevity and association with a single place affords them a particular insight on the spirit of landscape. Chloris Lowe, past President of the Ho-Chunk Nation, explains that in the Ho-Chunk tradition everything in the landscape and even material objects contain within them stories and the spirits of the people associated with them: "Everything has a life and a spirit. If your mother made a basket, part of her spirit went into that basket and remains within it." The same is true of the landscape, he notes. Whatever lands have been walked upon by ancestors—and especially those lands such as the Native American burial mounds that contain their bodies—retains their spirits. As a result, "The land is sacred. It is not that the landscape is not to be used, but that it is not to be abused. We are the caretakers. Think of how society treats a cemetery as a sacred place. Now lay that on the earth as a whole."[23]

Why did the mound-building end? Early archaeologists speculated that the mound-building people and their culture disappeared. But Millhouse and most modern archaeologists disagree. The end of mound-building was more likely due to cultural evolution, and the mound-building peoples are simply the ancestors of regional tribes such as the Ho-Chunk. Cemetery burial among the Native Americans eventually replaced mound-building.[24]

Albert has retreated to the pickup to take care of other duties while Sheila and I stroll among the bears. It is unseasonably warm today, and the bears appear to be basking in the cleared forest.

"Is it true that not all of the mounds host burials?" I ask. I have read that some, containing no known human remains, may have been ceremonial. But as we walk among the Marching Bears, Sheila hesitates to make an absolute distinction: "Even if no human remains have been detected in a mound, it's hard to say none were ever there." Some effigies, she explains, contained disarticulated remains instead of full skeletons; these as well as cremated human ashes could have disintegrated beyond detection.

I'm puzzled, too, how Euro-American explorers would have recognized these mounds centuries after they'd been overtaken by the forest. "The vegetation would have been different due to the looser soil on the mound compared to the surrounding soil," Sheila explains. "Often there are ferns and different native flowers on the mounds" that a trained eye could discern.

Still, most mounds went undetected or were purposely destroyed. Over 90 percent of Native American mounds have been plowed over or leveled for development since Euro-American settlement.

§ § §

We wander back to Albert in the pickup, and jostle back down the service road to the Effigy Mounds offices where LeBeau has something to show me. Although most mounds have been destroyed, either deliberately or

23. Lowe, Personal Interview.

24. Millhouse, Personal Interview.

unknowingly, undocumented mounds are occasionally still discovered, especially with LiDar technology. LiDar, LeBeau explains, is a "light-radar" that visually removes any covering above the ground surface, including buildings and tree and shrub cover. What is left is an image of the unblemished ground. With this image, any anomalies in the landscape—such as burial mounds—pop out to the eye.

LeBeau has some new mounds to show me, not far from the Marching Bears.

I sit dumbfounded, for on the screen in front of me this modern technology has turned the landscape to a living skin stretched tightly over the bones of earth. The skin of this landscape folds into creases and ravines like the palms of my hands, rises to fleshy hilltops, and slopes away around fingers.

And there, perhaps beneath a bony wrist, writhe bears and birds just under the taut skin.

If ever I felt that the earth breathes and has a spirit, it was then. The earth has a skin, with gigantic bears and birds burrowed beneath, just waiting for some untold spring to burst forth into a new day.

THE PORTAL

Dubliner Mary Gibbons felt the tug of her 5,000-year-old Irish ancestry as she stood in the dark center of the Newgrange Neolithic tomb watching the winter solstice sunrise spill up the passageway. Despite her resistance, she felt a spiritual link to the landscape and to the sun as well.

But how does someone like me find a spiritual landscape in a place where my family traces back only 140 years. For most Americans in their current locations, the historical connection to place is even thinner. How can a landscape be spiritual if I don't even know its stories?

The Effigy Mounds were built by an ancestry other than my own, by people whose stories are not my own (whose stories I tread carefully around, not wanting to appropriate them when so much more has been stolen). But even so, I take root where I can, and the Mounds are a starting place from which I begin to make my homeland spiritual.

And even closer to home, my perch above the Mississippi River at Dubuque is teaching me about spiritual landscapes. On this winter solstice with its grey sky blotting out the risen sun, the far shore may seem distant and the spring a long way off. But others have endured this necessary cold, and they are telling me that even though the land sleeps, it will soon enough reawaken. If there are marching bears and birds beneath its skin, they will stir and stretch and emerge, and all will return to life in the Thin Places.

Chapter 2

Imbolc: The Creation Is Good

IMBOLC, FEBRUARY 1

THE FEBRUARY 1 CELTIC feast of Imbolc [EE-molc] heralds the coming of spring to Ireland, but, like its secular, American cousin, Ground Hog Day, it seems a bit out of step with a Driftless calendar. Puxhatawnie Phil's pessimistic "six more weeks" would be an *early* end to winter for us here where the ground is still hard-frozen and our own Phils are fast asleep in their burrows.

Once again my sunrise Celtic feast—7:15 a.m. at the Julien Dubuque monument—is cold and gray. Dawn in such weather is not heralded by a trumpeting sun, but instead brightens slowly, sleepily. The morning awakens with a sigh that could well be the wind wheezing through the bare branches at the top of the bluff.

Below me, the Mississippi River is frozen solid, though pocked with occasional patches of open water bleeding through on the river bends where the current is quicker. These open waters will keep the bald eagles happy, providing them with fishing holes through all but the coldest weather. Maybe, just maybe, the open patches are spreading.

Imbolc comes from the Old Irish phrase "*i mbolg*," meaning "in the belly." As ewes approach the spring season for birthing, they begin lactating. The gathering sheep's milk is a reminder that after the long winter, the world's bounty will soon flow again. The creation is good and plentiful.

Imbolc is one of the four quarter-feasts in the Celtic year, falling halfway between the winter solstice and spring equinox. As with the solstices and equinoxes, the pre-Celtic Irish built megaliths aligned with the Imbolc sunrise. On Imbolc dawn, sunlight pours into a passage tomb called the Mound of the Hostages at the Hill of Tara, north of Dublin. Built as a passage tomb long before the arrival of Celtic culture, the Mound of the Hostages was repurposed to play a role in the coronation rite of Ireland's Celtic high kings. At the end of the coronation ceremony, after sitting upon the phallus-shaped stone called the Lia Fáil and having been found worthy, the new king entered the Mound of the Hostages in a symbolic mating with the earth goddess. If the king were good and just and generous during his reign, the earth would respond in kind, pouring forth its bounty. The king's sexual union with the earth goddess ensured bountiful harvests in the land.[1]

The early Celts dedicated the feast of Imbolc to the goddess Brigit. Sometimes portrayed as three sister goddesses who shared the same name, Brigit was the goddess of transformation—her name means "bridge." Brigit signals the transformation "of rock into metal, as goddess of smithcraft; of illness into health, as midwife goddess of healing; of ideas into art, as goddess of poetry,"[2] writes Patricia Monaghan in *The Red-Haired Girl from the Bog*. More related to spring (as the bridge from winter into summer), Brigit, the daughter of the earth-god Dagda, enables the land to bring forth its bounty.[3]

Brigit is likewise one of the key bridging figures from pre-Christianity into Christianity in Celtic Ireland. St. Brigit, whose feast is celebrated on her namesake goddess's feast, February 1, shares many of the same attributes as the goddess Brigit. Where the goddess had been the patron of poetry, the saint is the patron of the arts. Where the goddess hung her cloak on the sun, the saint was born to a "sunlike glow around her infant body."[4] Where the goddess Brigit is associated with fertility amid the birthing of the lambs, the saint calls forth abundance, coaxing milk cows to feed the poor from their bounty. Where the goddess is birth mother to Eriu, from whom Ireland takes its name, St. Brigit is also known as Ireland's Mary of the Gaels, the name Brigit in earlier times bestowed on infant girls as code for Mary, mother of Jesus.

1. O'Ríordáin, *The Music of What Happens*, 40.

2. Monaghan, *The Red-Haired Girl from the Bog*, 148.

3. Monaghan, *The Red-Haired Girl from the Bog*, 148.

4. Monaghan, *The Red-Haired Girl from the Bog*, 149.

The association of saint to goddess is so strong that some have questioned whether Saint Brigit was an actual person or simply a mythological goddess transformed into a mythological saint. But there appears to have been a fifth-century Brigit who was abbess of an important double monastery at Kildare, which would have given her the status and visibility to elevate her to sainthood. This Brigit was transformational in another regard (even if this "bridge" is not yet completed): legend tells that the Holy Spirit overtook the local bishop as he conferred Brigit's veil upon her head, whereupon he unwittingly read the rite conferring a bishop's rank upon her. When the conferring bishop was confronted about his "error," he replied, "I do not have any power in this matter. That dignity has been given by God to Brigit."[5]

The ordination could not be undone.

For it is February 1, and the slow northward roll of the sun cannot be undone. Lambs are in the bellies of the lactating ewes, and their quickening cannot be undone.

The creation is good and productive and bountiful, and it must not be undone.

THE RIVER SHANNON

My first encounter with the River Shannon took place during my first visit to Ireland, at the ruins of Clonmacnoise, a sixth-century monastery founded by St. Kieran, a lifelong friend of Glendalough's St. Kevin. Imbolc's promise of a bountiful spring and summer had come to fruition on a glorious August day in 2007, and as my wife and I walked amid the monastic ruins, high crosses, and round tower, we gazed out over a patch of blue sky and sparkling river that reminded me of home along the Mississippi.

The River Shannon gave birth to Clonmacnoise, as Kieran chose to settle at the point where east-west eskers—the ancient, elevated, glacially-produced walking paths across the midland bogs—intersected with the general north-south flow of Ireland's longest river. Clonmacnoise's location on the river nourished its rise to a major center of worship and learning that lasted until the twelfth century. But the Shannon also fed the monastery's decline, as the river provided easy access for enemies: seven raids from invading Vikings, six from the colonizing Normans, and even more numerous attacks by competing factions of Irish petty (local) kings.

5. Sellner, *Wisdom of the Celtic Saints*, 72.

The River Shannon runs about 220 miles, starting from a pool called the Shannon Pot at the base of Tiltinbane Mountain in northwest Ireland's County Cavan. The Shannon then bisects Ireland—much like North America's Mississippi River—spilling into several natural and dam-enhanced lakes before turning west and emptying into an 80-mile estuary at Limerick en route to its union with the Atlantic Ocean.

The Shannon takes its name from the Celtic goddess Sínann [SHE-non], who aspired to wisdom by eating the salmon that swam bountifully at the headwater pool of the as-yet-unformed river. The salmon themselves had ingested wisdom by eating the nuts that fell into the pool from the surrounding hazel trees, the Celtic tree of knowledge. Forbidden as a woman to eat the salmon from the well, Sínann did so anyway. Wisdom immediately coursed through her veins, but the well waters arose and burst from their confines in a raging flood, drowning Sínann and sweeping her downstream and out to sea. Thereafter, the waters never returned to the confines of the well, and the River Shannon was born.

In *The Encyclopedia of Celtic Mythology and Folklore*, Patricia Monaghan disputes an anti-feminist reading of the myth, arguing, "Although often interpreted as a cautionary tale, warning women against seeking wisdom, Sínann's story can also be seen as a creation myth, in which she sacrifices herself to establish the land's fertility."[6] Monaghan views Sínann's story as an act of "dissolving of her divine power into the water, which then gives life to the land."[7]

Quite so. In pre-modern times, tens of thousands of salmon weighing forty pounds or more would rush upriver each spring to spawn. The Shannon floodplain also nourishes marshes, grasslands, and bogs with abundant wildlife, including egrets, coots, herring gulls, feral goats, otters, kingfishers, giant butterflies and dragonflies. Meanwhile the Shannon estuary with its tidal flats and open water is home to whooper's swan, graylag goose, whales, seals—to 50,000 species all told.

But given its strategic central location, the River Shannon has also been a prime target for military and industrial use, which has, over the centuries, put its teeming wildlife at risk. Invading Vikings and Normans penetrated inland along the Shannon's waters, local kings used the Shannon for war-time transportation, and Irish rebels slipped across the Shannon for refuge from British colonial armies. Developers, meanwhile, siphoned

---

6. Monaghan, *The Encyclopedia of Celtic Mythology and Folklore*, 420.

7. Monaghan, *The Encyclopedia of Celtic Mythology and Folklore*, 27.

some of its waters toward Dublin via the Grand Canal in 1759 and the Royal Canal in 1817 for movement of goods. Thirteen locks raise and lower commercial tows along the often-shallow river, which drops only 60 feet in its first 140 miles. Disruption of the natural flow of the river contributes to siltation. And a hydroelectric plant built in the late 1920s at Ardnacrusha in southwest Ireland's County Clare further disrupts the natural river.

The Old River Shannon Research Group calls the Shannon Hydroelectric Scheme "the greatest ecological disaster in Ireland."[8] Although a canal diverts water to the hydroelectric dam miles away from the river, the diversion decreases the river's volume, which in turn has degraded wetlands, fish habitat, and salmon runs. To maintain a workable flow of water to the dam through the drier summer months, smaller upstream dams retain winter and spring runoff in several lakes, leading to habitat degradation in those locations as well.

A host of other modern developments likewise challenge the ecological health of the River Shannon: drainage of wetlands for agriculture, forestry, and municipal construction; city and industrial pollutants; agricultural runoff; dikes, bridges, and culverts; invasive species brought in by commercial vessels; and navigational dredging.[9] Recent years have brought record amounts of rainfall—even for Ireland—and flooding has been recurrent along the Shannon. Communities are preparing to wrestle with Shannon flooding into the indefinite future, in anticipation of global climate change.

Despite these challenges, the River Shannon holds on as one of Ireland's ecological treasures teeming with life. New organizations, initiatives, and protections have helped its cause, such as the private Old River Shannon Trust, the governmental Shannon River Basin District, and the establishment of the Lower River Shannon Special Area of Conservation to help protect habitat of bottlenose dolphins, sea lampreys, mussels, and numerous seabird species.[10] Salmon runs constructed at locks and dams help the leaping fish return upstream for the spawning season, and water screens at the Ardnacrusha dam have helped protect the eel population.

The Brigit of the feast of Imbolc, the goddess and saint of transformations, provided a bridge from the dead of winter to the rebirth of spring.

8. Old River Shannon Research Group.
9. Old River Shannon Research Group.
10. Shannon Dolphin and Wildlife Foundation.

The goddess Sínann meanwhile transformed the Irish midlands, offering her life to bring wisdom and bounty and the River Shannon itself to the landscape.

Nature is bursting and the creation is good.

On that first visit to the River Shannon at Clonmacnoise, Dianne and I left the monastic ruins behind and wandered toward the river shore, drawn by the twisted contortions of the Norman-built Clonmacnoise castle ruins whose walls tumbled in on themselves after its destruction by Irish rebels near the turn of the fourteenth century. It appeared at first that we could circle the castle by walking gingerly across a shoreline mudflat that caressed the castle's backside along the river. Dianne took the first step, and plunged a white tennis shoe deep into the black silt.

It might have been Iowa mud, Driftless mud, given its deep, dark texture. It was a rich, gooey gumbo that offered itself up, nearby, to blazing green river reeds waving against a blue sky.

THE CREATION IS GOOD

On Easter Sunday, I treat myself to a drive to the twelfth-century Cong Abbey ruins on the County Mayo/Galway border, a favorite site from my prior visits to Ireland. A short distance from the monastic campus sits the Monks' Fishing House, a small stone hut thrust from the shoreline out into the River Cong. Monks could drop a fishing line or net through a rectangular hole in the limestone floor that opened into the swift-flowing river. A rope running from the hut to a bell back at the monastery allowed the fishing monks to alert the kitchen of their successes.

The River Cong that rushes past the fishing hut arises like a miracle out of the limestone at the adjacent village, and flows for just one mile until it spills into nearby Lough Corrib. But its real source is Lough Mask a few miles northwest. From Lough Mask the waters disappear into at least five underground flows that converge and emerge back into daylight at the village of Cong.

Sitting in a stone hut in spring, catching the wise salmon almost literally from beneath your feet as they swim up a river that emerges full-strength from the nearby stones—how easy it is to say that the Creation is good.

Need it be more complicated than this?

§ § §

In a seminal 1967 essay titled "The Historical Roots of Our Ecological Crisis," medieval historian Lynn White, Jr., took Christianity to task for establishing destructive western attitudes toward nature that persist today and which lie at the heart of modern environmental problems. White argues that because the Bible puts so much emphasis on humans having been created in the likeness of God, "Christianity is the most anthropocentric religion the world has seen."[11] Humans in the Bible, as well as their creating God, transcend nature, instead of existing within it.

White contrasts Christianity with indigenous religions, saying:

> In Antiquity every tree, every spring, every stream, every hill had its own genius loci, its guardian spirit . . . Before one cut a tree, mined a mountain, or dammed a brook, it was important to placate the spirit in charge of that particular situation, and to keep it placated. By destroying pagan animism, Christianity made it possible to exploit nature.[12]

The Judeo-Christian creation story draws particular criticism from environmentalists. In the Genesis story, says White, God planned the creation "explicitly for man's benefit and rule: no item in the physical creation had any purpose save to serve man's purposes."[13] Thus on the sixth "day" of creation, God tells his newly created humans, "Fill the earth and subdue it. Rule over the fish in the sea and the birds in the sky and over every living creature that moves on the ground."[14] Genesis 2 likewise draws environmental criticism for giving Adam the power to name the animals, thus bestowing upon the human race yet another power of dominion.

No doubt Christianity has deserved much of this line of environmental criticism. In the second century, the Christian Gnostic movement, deriving from Platonic dualism, dichotomized the world into physical and spiritual realms. In doing so, Gnostics argued that if the spiritual world was eternal and good, then the physical, created world must be temporary and debased. The body, as part of the physical world, must likewise be decadent and corrupt. Gnosticism was denounced as heresy when Gnostics took the

---

11. White, "The Historical Roots of Our Ecologic Crisis," 1206.

12. White, "The Historical Roots of Our Ecologic Crisis," 1206.

13. White, "The Historical Roots of Our Ecologic Crisis," 1206.

14. *Catholic Family Edition of the Holy Bible*, Genesis 1: 22.

argument one step further and claimed, by extension, that the divine Jesus must not have been truly human.

Although repudiated, the gnostic mindset (and Greco-Roman dualism in general) continued to have a back-door influence on lived Christian experience, if not on theology per se. Catholicism, for example, has long found itself conflicted over the holiness of the physical world. On the one hand, Catholicism is a deeply carnal religion, offering a bloodied Christ in crucifixion and a risen Christ who invites Thomas to probe his wounds with his fingers. Culturally, Catholicism has been more open than many of its cousin denominations to celebrate the fruits of the earth—wines and breads and meats and fishes. David Toolan, SJ, writes, "Catholicism, if it does its job, keeps us close to bodily experience. Traditionally, it has aimed to be a sensuous faith, and behind its use of earth, air, fire, and water in its rites lies a rich sense of the sacramentality of the universe as a whole . . . At root, this is an experiential matter."[15]

Yet denial and suppression of the human body has likewise been long associated with the Catholic tradition. From sexual repression to mortification, Catholicism has taught the faithful to be wary of bodily pleasure.

And if the body is not to be celebrated, why then should its physical cousin, the earth? Early Protestantism, meanwhile, emboldened the onslaught of the earth through other means. Protestantism championed the historical origins of individualism and capitalism, which at their extremes have led to resource depletion and exploitation.

While valid to a degree, such arguments that the Judeo-Christian tradition established anti-environmental habits of mind overlook other aspects of the tradition that celebrate and honor nature. In Leviticus, God dispels any notion that the Creation serves only human consumption, saying, "Mine is the land." Here God directs the Israelites to give the land occasional rest, to let the land lie fallow every seventh year.[16] And in the much maligned Genesis creation story, God looks back at end of each day's labor and calls it "good" even before creating humans. The refrain bears repeating:

> And *God saw the light was good* . . .
> And God called the dry *land* Earth; and the gathering together of the waters called the Seas: and *God saw that it was good* . . .

15. Toolan, "The Voice of the Hurricane," 68.
16. Burbery, "Ecocriticism and Christian Literary Scholarship," 199.

And the earth brought forth grass, *and* herbs and all kinds of trees: and *God saw that it was good* . . .

And to rule over the day and over the night, and to divide the light from the darkness: and *God saw that it was good* . . .

And God created great whales, and every living creature that moveth, which the waters brought forth abundantly, after their kind, and every winged fowl after his kind: and *God saw that it was good* . . .

And God made all kinds of wild beasts, every kind of cattle, and every kind of creature crawling on the ground: and *God saw that it was good* . . . [17] (Italics added)

Sr. Kathleen O'Neill, a Cistercian Trappist nun from Our Lady of the Mississippi Abbey near my home in Dubuque, likewise defends Genesis' "dominion" passage: "Only a modern society that has most of nature under 'control' would be bothered by the terms 'dominion' and 'subdue.' At the time Genesis was written, it was simply a daunting task to survive in nature, and so these words were encouragement to not be overwhelmed." O'Neill adds, "That doesn't mean it doesn't break my heart to hear of the Amazon forest being felled." [18]

Sister Kathleen believes that land is sacred, spiritual, and sacramental. "First, as a believer in a Creator, I view the creation as God's work. It's not an accident, it's not our doing, and it's not entirely our 'garden.' Nature has an integrity all its own. Second, nature is a great manifestation of beauty, and beauty is a manifestation of God. The beauty of nature speaks of God without any help from us."[19]

The directive God gives to Adam and Eve to tend the Garden of Eden is conventionally referred to as the stewardship passage. The stewardship of Eden, too, is typically maligned by a modern environmental reading as putting humans "in charge" of the Earth, establishing a hierarchy placing humans above nature. But as Larry Rasmussen points out in *Earth Community, Earth Ethics*, "The steward is the one entrusted with things precisely *not* his or her own."[20] A land steward is, by definition, precisely *not* the owner, and as such is not free to do with the earth simply as she or he pleases.

---

17. *Catholic Family Edition of the Holy Bible*, Genesis I: 3-25

18. O'Neill, Personal Interview.

19. O'Neill, Personal Interview.

20. Rasmussen, *Earth Community, Earth Ethics*, 68

Anne M. Clifford, CSJ, argues that even the task given to Adam of naming the animals did not give Adam dominion over them, but instead established a personal relationship between Adam and the animals: "Naming is reflective of how human persons establish relationships with other creatures and with God. From an ecological standpoint, the activity of naming is one way in which humans express the bond that they have with nonhuman creatures."[21]

Two Francis's from Christendom likewise implore us to put ourselves in right relationship to the creation. St. Francis of Assisi writes, in his "Canticle of All Creatures":

> Praised be You my Lord with all Your creatures,
> especially Sir Brother Sun,
> Who is the day through whom You give us light.
> And he is beautiful and radiant with great splendor,
> Of You Most High, he bears the likeness.
>
> Praised be You, my Lord, through Sister Moon and the stars.
> In the heavens you have made them bright, precious and fair.
>
> Praised be You, my Lord, through Brothers Wind and Air.
> And fair and stormy, all weather's moods,
> by which You cherish all that You have made.
>
> Praised be You my Lord through Sister Water,
> So useful, humble, precious and pure.
>
> Praised be You my Lord through Brother Fire,
> through whom You light the night
> and he is beautiful and playful and robust and strong.
>
> Praised be You my Lord through our Sister,
> Mother Earth who sustains and governs us,
> producing varied fruits with coloured flowers and herbs.

A Creation described in terms of human family relations offers no one sibling dominion. Instead of simply serving humans, the Creation gives glory to God simply by being.

---

21. Clifford, "Foundations for a Catholic Ecological Theology of God," 25.

Eight hundred years later, Pope Francis, in his encyclical *Laudato Sí*, echoes his namesake in proclaiming that non-human creatures have value unto themselves: "In our time, the Church does not simply state that other creatures are completely subordinated to the good of human beings, as if they have no worth in themselves and can be treated as we wish. . . . Each creature possesses its own particular goodness and perfection."[22]

But if the Creation is good, then what do we make of this goodness when the creation comes crashing at our doorstep with famine, flood, drought, or disease? Are we still looking at the goodness of God, or are we now into the materialists' world of an uncaring universe? Perhaps the answer lies in looking beyond the anthropocentric notion that the creation exists solely for the human race. Even destructive forces like fire and flood renew the face of the earth.

§ § §

On a wintry January morning I meet Chloris Lowe, past President of the Ho-Chunk Nation, in the lobby of the Ho-Chunk Nation headquarters in La Crosse, Wisconsin. Chloris is sitting on a couch joking with another tribal member inside the sprawling building that was once a Masonic Temple. He laughs with a receptionist as we procure a room in which to talk, and pauses briefly to introduce me to a woman who relates some of her recent political activity.

Once settled into our seats, Chloris is soon telling me a creation story, one told to him through an interpreter by a tribal person from the Amazon, but which echoes the creation stories of many North and South American tribes.

Outside there is a deep snow, but inside I am warm and spellbound. The story-teller begins:

In the beginning, in the first creation, the Creator created the birds, mammals, and other creatures, but not man. The animals lived in community and could talk to each other. They had been given everything they needed for life and didn't have to hunt and eat each other. But each had been given a particular responsibility in the community, and at the end of each day the Creator called a Grand Council with all the animals. Each animal would step forth and explain what she/he had done for the community that day.

---

22. Pope Francis, *Laudato Sí*, Parag. 69.

After a while, some of the animals began to say that they had done a little more than others. They began to believe that they were just a little better and more important. All of the animals belittled the turtle as the lowest and least important among the creatures. The turtle, they said, did not contribute much to the good of the community. One day the eagle said in derision, "I can see into the future. When I fly high above the earth, I can see what the turtle will not see until tomorrow because it crawls low on the ground."

The Creator watched all of this and said, "This is not what I wanted the world to be. I will end this." So he sent a great flood that covered all of the earth. The animals died off. The eagle had no place to land, and eventually plunged into the sea and died. For eons, the sea was like a great mirror, dead still, without a ripple on its surface.

Then the Creator decided to make a second Creation. He called for some clay to be brought up from the bottom of the sea. Finally, the surface of the sea rippled. The turtle—the only being that the Creator had saved— had swum up from the bottom of the sea with a lump of clay on its back.

The Creator took the clay and once again formed the land and re-created the animals, but this time without the ability to speak. And now they would have to subsist on one another, to become hunter and hunted. The Creator told them why they had been so reduced.

Then the Creator made woman and man from the clay. He showed them the animals and said, "These are your brothers and sisters who did not live their lives as they should have. You are to be their caretaker. But learn from them what they did wrong."

Over time, the humans began to act as the first animals had acted, some thinking themselves more important than others. So the Creator divided the humans into four groups and dispersed them in the four directions of the earth. He gave each group one responsibility to learn—earth, fire, wind, and water—and told them that there would not be peace on earth, nor could they come together in unity, until each group had learned its responsibility.

And here Chloris returns to the tiny room in the Ho-Chunk headquarters in La Crosse, and brings me with him. "One group," he says again, "was told to master fire. And we are still trying to wrestle with fire today. We only need to look to global warming to see we have not mastered fire."[23]

---

23. Lowe, Personal Interview.

§ § §

The Creation is good, but maybe not as we understand the good. Evolution created no special privileges for humans, other than larger than average brains, a better than average ability to communicate, and opposable thumbs. With these we have made a place in the world and endangered it as well.

Even if a Creator singled out the human race to tend the garden and be responsible to the earth community, this still bestowed no ownership or the right to despoil. The earth provides for us—otherwise we would no longer be here—but it provides for all other species as well, and its goodness is not measured solely against human wants and needs.

§ § §

I am a monk sitting in a fifteenth-century fishing house on the River Cong, I am a salmon on the River Shannon swimming upstream, I am the Shannon relentlessly flooding, the River Cong bursting forth from the limestone. I am a turtle with mud on my back, I am Brigit and Sínann transforming the earth, a lactating ewe urging forth new life. I am Imbolc on a Mississippi River bluff swathed in winter grey but knowing that the spring will come, knowing that the sun is pushing it along, and knowing that none of it can be held back.

THE MISSISSIPPI RIVER

On a mid-June afternoon, Dianne and I drop a tandem kayak into the Mississippi River backwaters at the Galena Ferry Landing and paddle upstream. Here on the Harris Slough, cut off from the channel by a maze of interlacing, forested berms, we are largely protected from currents and motor boats. In our kayak we pass swiftly and silently across the just-blooming water lilies, reach the far end of the slough, grab a beverage from the cooler and float for a while back downstream.

Even so, two days ago a storm had dropped five inches of rain, and the chocolate brown river is on the rise. There is an urgency in the flow, even in the backwaters, an awakening that commands our respect.

The Mississippi River stretches 2,300 miles from tiny Lake Itasca in northern Minnesota to the Gulf of Mexico. Along with its two most significant tributaries—the Missouri and the Ohio Rivers—it drains about

40 percent of the continental United States from the Rocky Mountains to western New York State. The Mississippi discharges 420 billion gallons of river water into the Gulf of Mexico each day.[24]

The Upper Mississippi National Wildlife and Fish Refuge waters on which we're kayaking constitute only slightly more than 10 percent of the river's length. Covering 261 miles from Wabasha, MN, to Rock Island, IL, the Refuge roughly coincides with the western border of the Driftless Land. It protects 240,000 acres of floodplain, and is by many measures the most biologically diverse section of the river. One hundred miles above the Refuge, the river is still fairly small (although undammed and therefore more natural); below the Refuge, large sections of the river are hemmed in shore to shore by dikes. In between, the Upper Mississippi Refuge, with its forested bluffs jutting up to six hundred feet above the river, hosts 306 bird species, 250 bald eagle nests, 5,000 heron and egret nests, 50 percent of the world's canvasback ducks, 51 mammal species, forty-two mussel species, and 111 species of fish. Forty percent of the nation's waterfowl use the Mississippi, including the refuge, as their migration highway in spring and fall.[25]

The Mississippi we know today took shape during the melting of the most recent glaciers 10,000 to 12,000 years ago, although older iterations had once coursed through its valleys or nearby. Glacial meltwater—aided by the sudden bursting of upstream ice dams—carved the deep bluffs of the Upper Mississippi through the Driftless. As the meltwater subsided and the ocean levels rose, the river slowed, ceased down-cutting, dropped its glacial till on the river floor, and settled somewhat calmly into meandering paths far beneath the corridor bluffs.

The Upper Mississippi provided a refuge for Native Americans hunting megafauna just beyond the glaciers' reach as early as twelve thousand years ago. It was home to Native Americans until shortly after 1832, the end of the Black Hawk War, when most tribes were forcibly removed from its shores.

The Ojibwe had called it *Misi-ziibi*, the Great River, which the French rendered into *Messipi*. The first European-Americans to enter the Upper Mississippi, starting from the Great Lakes and portaging to the Wisconsin River, were the crew of Jacques Marquette and Louis Joliet in 1673.

---

24. Fremling, *Immortal River*, 13-16.

25. U.S. Fish & Wildlife Service.

Marquette kept a journal, in which he describes at last entering the Mississippi at the mouth of the Wisconsin:

> Here we are, then, on this so renowned River . . . It is narrow at the place where the Miskous [Wisconsin] empties; its Current, which flows southward, is slow and gentle. To the right is a large Chain of very high Mountains, and to the left are beautiful lands; in various Places, the stream is Divided by Islands.[26]

In late September I stop at Pike's Peak State Park on the Iowa bluff, 450 feet above the river across from the confluence of the Wisconsin and Mississippi that Marquette described. Halfway between Lock & Dam #9 at Lynxville, Wisconsin, and #10 at Guttenberg, Iowa, the river here most resembles its natural flow, and I am seeing roughly the same interlocking chain of islands that Marquette described.

Later, across the river in Prairie du Chien, I drop in at the office of Richard King,[27] then-manager of the Upper Mississippi Wildlife Refuge's McGregor District. The Refuge is divided into four such districts, the McGregor being the largest at ninety-eight river miles and the second from the south. This stretch, King explains, has phenomenal mussel resources like the federally protected Higgins Eye Pearly mussel, the largest waterfowl migration numbers, the best intact flood plain forests, and double the number of bald eagles compared to other districts.

Most people who live in the cities and towns along the Upper Mississippi, who occasionally watch the barges lumber past, and who vaguely understand the workings of the locks and dams would never guess that a wildlife refuge exists amid this river traffic. King points out that this is probably because one of the Upper Mississippi Refuge's more unique features is that it's a "working river." The Refuge was established in 1924 to support wildlife and fish habitat in the aftermath of an aborted Department of Agriculture proposal to line the Upper Mississippi with levees such as one finds in the Lower Mississippi today. The levees would have more narrowly constricted the river, with lowlands—former wetlands—beyond the levees to be repurposed for agriculture. Had this taken place, the floodplains and backwaters of today's river would not exist.

At the same time, however, the Refuge's enabling legislation restricted its environmental oversight by saying it could not interfere with navigation.

26. Marquette, *The Mississippi Voyage of Jolliet and Marquette*, 236.

27. King, Personal Interview.

The Refuge remained neutral when the locks and dams were installed to support barge navigation in the 1930s. Twenty-nine dams along the Upper Mississippi reconfigured the river into a series of flat pools descending in staircase fashion from one pool to the next downstream. The locks act as elevators raising and lowering barges and other boats as they head north or south.

Before the dams were built, water levels could vary greatly in the backwaters from year to year and season to season, a variation that actually kept the wetlands healthy by allowing vegetation to take hold in dry seasons. Today the dams keep the backwaters perpetually wet, ironically decreasing their productivity as wildlife habitat. In addition, since water moves more slowly through the pooled backwaters, sediment from farm fields, excavation sites, and nearby towns settles out as a rising mud floor across the sloughs.

"Rivers are supposed to go through droughts and floods," laying bare the shores and cutting off backwaters in dry periods and flooding the riverine forests in high water, King explains. "But this river is locked in." While low waters and flooding still occur, both extremes are mitigated by the control of water levels behind the dams. The result is good for human structures downstream from the dam but bad for wetlands.

Islands are subject to erosion as winds whip up the lake-like pools immediately above each dam. "I've given tours to people in their 50s and 60s, and they'll point out where entire islands have disappeared" in the pools behind the dams, says King.

The Mississippi faces a host of environmental threats as relentless as the river's flow. Invasive species dragged in by international shipping plague native species and habitats alike. Tiny invasive zebra mussels grow prolifically on the shells of native mollusks and eventually starve them. Invasive milfoil seaweed spreads thickly over the backwaters, choking out native plants and degrading fish habitat.

If some pollution comes from upriver, plenty more is sent downstream. Iowa's tributaries, for example, carry some of the most fertilizer-laden water in the U.S., which the Mississippi carries to the Gulf of Mexico, contributing to a 6,500-square-mile Dead Zone in the Gulf of Mexico upon arrival.

But as with the River Shannon, the Mississippi River has been fighting back with the help of public and private initiatives. The Army Corps of Engineers has constructed new river islands made resistant to erosion with riprap. King's own Refuge conservation projects include forest restoration. "In many stretches of the river, only the silver maple can survive prolonged inundation due to the locks and dams," he says, so the Refuge is working to preserve the few oak forests that have survived and to plant oaks in drier areas. Nearby Cassville High School and Lansing Middle School sixth grade students have helped to plant these oak forests. King says, "I consider these efforts to be successful for two reasons: one, we will have some new oak forests in future years; and two, it is engaging and empowering kids who take pride in their work and return to see how 'their trees' are doing and hopefully become more attuned to environmental issues in their future adult lives."

King seems personally more comfortable talking about policies, projects, and habitat than about the quality of life the river provides. But as we near the end of our conversation he adds, "I live on the river. My grandkids and I spend time on the river. It's part of who I am and who they are. Passing that legacy on to them is important to me."

§ § §

The Paris Treaty of 1783 that ended the American War of Independence established the Mississippi River as the western boundary of the United States, setting off a rush to find the headwaters in order to firmly establish the border. Surveyors David Thompson, Zebulon Pike, Lewis Cass, and Giacomo Beltrami each took their turn searching for the headwaters from 1798 through 1823, each settling on a different Minnesota lake as the source. In 1832 Henry Rowe Schoolcraft was the first to employ Native Americans in the quest, and the Ojibwe guide Ozawindib led him to what the Ojibwe called Elk Lake and which Schoolcraft promptly renamed as Lake Itasca by combining parts of the Latin words for "truth" and "head," *verITAS CAput*. The odd combination reflected the practice at the time of creating new names that "sounded Indian" but weren't.

The Ojibwe, meanwhile, were bemused by Schoolcraft's and his predecessors' obsession over finding the headwaters. According to Larry Aitken, Leech Lake Reservation Historian, "To Indians, it was amusing, that aggressive effort . . . Because [to us], it was not important where it started—the whole river was of central importance."[28]

Regardless of accuracy, Itasca has been recognized as the Mississippi headwaters ever since. In 1891 it was enshrined as the center and namesake

28. Lake Itasca State Park Information Center.

of Minnesota's first state park that today covers 32,500 acres and attracts half a million visitors each year. For most, the highlight will be walking across the fledgling shin-deep river as it emerges from Lake Itasca.

About six weeks after I returned from Ireland, I vacationed with my extended family on another lake in north-central Minnesota. One windy day when our lake wasn't hospitable to kayaking, my wife, daughter and I took a day-trip north to Lake Itasca to see the headwaters, far to the north of our Driftless home.

Here the glaciers that bypassed the Driftless Land had left their mark: glacial plains south of Itasca State Park, hilly moraines that the great ice lobes had bulldozed, eskers, and, of course, the glacial lakes themselves.

And here began our Mississippi River, clean, clear, and tumbling forth from Lake Itasca over a cascade of rounded stones, pushing with a force as light as lambs but no less determined and no less unstoppable.

And here in the fifteen-foot-wide river with its glacially-pebbled bottom played not salmon but children.

And the Creation was good.

THE PORTAL

On the February feast of Imbolc, the Mississippi River is still frozen while I wait for the sky to brighten on a cloud-filled dawn.

There are no bird sounds at the dawn of February, only the sighing of wind through the bare branches. How can there be life here?

But beneath the ice, the Mississippi still flows, as if in a Thin Place. The sun is inching northward and pulling Spring behind it. The ice will break up, the birds return, the oaks bud out. Winter clouds will give way to blue sky.

In Ireland the salmon will leap, the sheep will lamb. The River Shannon will bathe the shore of Clonmacnoise.

Chapter 3

Spring Equinox: The Holy Transforms the Familiar

SPRING EQUINOX

I HAD BEGUN TO think I was still in Ireland after my first two Celtic dawn pilgrimages to the Julien Dubuque Monument. Each time the cloud-choked morning only slightly lightened to an unpolished steely gray. But finally on the spring equinox a purple sky ripened to pink and spread across the horizon.

The March 21 equinox is the astronomical beginning of Spring, as its September twin heralds the start of Fall. In the Driftless, however, true Spring still lies just beyond the equinox. The soil today is thawed and loamy, but the oak woods is still winter-brown. Beneath the bluff, small ice slushes mottle the river, riding the current south.

But on the horizon across the river, now, suddenly—absent one moment and now visible the next—crowns a tiny orange ball of sun.

And, to my total surprise, as the rising sun clears the horizon, it fills the interior of Dubuque's grave with a vibrant, orange glow, casting a shadow of the iron gates across the back wall of the monument. My Newgrange in miniature.

The Holy transforms the familiar.

GLENDALOUGH

Stone-slabbed tombstones and weather-beaten Celtic crosses lean askew among the ruins of the monastic city. The tumbled walls at Glendalough [GLEN-da-lock] proclaim the rise and fall of Ireland's Golden Age of Saints and Scholars more than a thousand years ago. But I have not met anyone who hasn't felt this place curiously alive and still-transformed today.

Glendalough, located thirty miles south of Dublin, means Valley of the Two Lakes in Irish. The ruins rest at the end of a narrow, glacially scooped valley flanked by 500-foot tall semi-forested ridges, an oasis of green in the rocky and bog-strewn Wicklow Mountains. Just beyond the edge of the monastic city lie the shores of the Upper and Lower Lakes with their clear mountain waters reflecting the sharp slopes of the cliff walls.

St. Kevin, or Coemgen [CAVE-yin], chose this valley for his monastery in the sixth century, just a few generations after the Christianization of Ireland. Why he selected this particular mountain glen among all others in the Wicklow Mountains is uncertain. The mountain streams that feed and exit the twin lakes are unnavigable. The site itself lies deep inside the Wicklow Mountains, not at the edges where it might be more accessible. Even so, it projects none of the austerity of the wind-battered rocks of Skellig Michael or the Aran Islands where some of the early Celtic Christian monks subjected themselves to nature's harshest blows. If anything, Glendalough drew its energy from nature's lavish abundance, with fish in the lakes and wild deer and boar in the forested slopes. There is both bounty and beauty here, with a mountain stream cascading down the slopes and winding through the valley floor toward the lakes amid moss-draped yews and oaks.

Perhaps a clue to the monastery's location—if a clue at all—comes from *The Metrical Life of St. Kevin*, which simply states that he "crossed the summits with an angel and built a monastery among the glens."[1] The clue lies not in the reference to an angel—which you may believe in or reject as you wish—but lies instead in the inexplicability of the particular choice of site above all others.

Why here, why not there?

At Glendalough, Kevin initially lived as a hermit in a cave above the Upper Lake already sacred to pre-Christians as a rock-hewn Bronze-Age tomb. Eventually he called other monks to the glen and established the

---

1. Rodgers and Losack. *Glendalough: A Celtic Pilgrimage*, 11.

Glendalough monastery, although Kevin still occasionally retreated to his solitary cave (now called St. Kevin's Bed) and to another small monastic hut about halfway up the mountainside.

Glendalough grew to become a major center of religion and learning, a "monastic city" of monks, lay peasants, and surrounding landed patrons. The monastery transformed the sleepy valley into a typically active monastic web of agriculture, smithcraft, education, scribing and artistic illumination of religious texts, and prayer. Within the monastic enclosure a visitor would likely have found a kitchen, infirmary, scriptorium, library, guesthouse, monks' living quarters, and numerous small chapels. And since early Christian Celtic lay monks were often married, the monastic city may have been diverse and lively with women and children.[2]

Glendalough also became a pilgrimage site after Kevin's death. The tradition may have started with Kevin and his friend Kieran of Clonmacnoise on the banks of the River Shannon, both of whom are said to have travelled miles across the mountains and midland eskers to visit each other. In the ensuing centuries, an east-west footpath through the Wicklow Gap became a pilgrimage route, perhaps following sections of Kevin's trail.

From such monasteries came the learned men and women of Ireland's Golden Age, from the fifth to the ninth century. They were the secretaries and printing presses of the day, writing histories of the pre-Christian Celts and copying Christian holy books with exquisitely scrolled artwork. They brought Christianity back to the European continent after the Roman Empire's collapse.

But trouble lurked on the horizon. Vikings sacked the monastic city for gold vessels and other treasure several times between 900 and 1100 AD. Glendalough survived these plundering raids, but finally met its end at the hands of the Anglo-Normans. The armies of King Richard II destroyed the monastery in 1398, fearing the potential rivalry of an Irish center of learning amid the spreading Anglo-Norman seats of power.

Then Glendalough entered its long sleep. Locals buried their dead among the decaying walls. Today the Round Tower, St. Kevin's Church, the Gateway, the Cathedral, and several other structures serve as reminders of the Golden Age. Some retain only remnants of their original walls, while others have been reconstructed.

Now it is the forested hills and the clear lakes that give Glendalough life. The 80-mile Wicklow Way hiking trail crosses the mountainsides to the

2. Rodgers and Losack, *Glendalough: A Celtic Pilgrimage*, 40-41.

north and south, bringing more secular pilgrims to the ruins. A mountain ridge trail encircles the lakes on a boardwalk spanning rock outcrops, bog, forest, and mountain streams. St. Kevin's Way cuts through the Wicklow Gap for nineteen miles to the west, roughly following the ancient pilgrimage path.

Visitors to Glendalough National Park are equally mesmerized by the monastic ruins and the setting that cradles it. The sanctuary stone with its rough-cut cross that lies inside the arched-stone gateway announces, as it has for more than a millennium, entry to a place of peace. The mountain stream footbridges and the lakeside walking path complete the effect.

Another hiking trail leads from the monastic city halfway up the mountainside to St. Kevin's Cell, a still-removed but less severely hermetic site than his cave bed. Here legend has it that Kevin cradled a nesting blackbird in the palm of his outstretched hand for weeks until her young hatched and flew away. The apocryphal story no doubt points to his love of nature.

But the poet Seamus Heaney imagines Kevin morphing into the landscape itself during the ordeal. The pain of aching knees and arm held aloft subsides as Kevin is subsumed into bedrock, trunk, and branch.[3]

Glendalough has mesmerized, awed, and calmed me with my every visit to the site. But a different view of the monastic city struck me recently during a guided hike through the nearby Brockagh Mountains. On the day after my arrival in Dublin, I was hillwalking, as the Irish call it, in the Wicklow Mountains with Russ Mills, a mountaineering expert.[4] Our walk began at Glendalough, but we quickly climbed upward from the valley of the monastic ruins and ascended toward nearby Brochagh Mountain. It would be several hours until we saw Glendalough again from a distance.

I was Russ' only customer on a midweek morning, so he tailored his commentary to my personal interests, which this day seemed focused on bedrock, to Russ' delight as he got to dust off his undergraduate geology degree. On the ascent I'd been admiring some tightly-layered and colorful outcrops that Russ identified as mica schists, a metamorphic rock pressurized from mud shales into tortured, sparkling twists by the heat and pressure of continental collision. Occasional white bursts of quartzite punctuated the layers, a mineral brine likewise boiled up from deep inside the earth.

3. Heaney, Seamus, *Opened Ground, Collected Poems*, 384.

4. Russel Mills is the owner/operator of Mountaintrails, a guided hiking service. Mills also trains others in certified mountaineering.

Up ahead he pointed to where a field of granite began, a molten sub-surface flow that hardened 400 million years ago and gradually reached the surface by erosion of the layers above it.[5] Touching the granular igneous rock, it occurred to me that this is it, this where the magma flow ended, here, this hill, not the next one over.

Suddenly I was confronted by the "this-ness" of the earth: the landscape may stretch out in vast swaths before one's eyes and hurdle into unseen lands as well, but right here, at this place, a lava flow stopped cold in its tracks 400 million years ago and emerged on the landscape as a granite outcrop.

And the angel said, here, not there.

Our solitary hike continued across the boggy mountaintop, past glacial erratic boulders and with far-off views of a snow-capped mountain. We talked about Russ' mountaineering business, about politics, history, and culture. Sometimes there was only the comfortable silence of two middle-aged men walking together at a brisk pace across the mountain bog, not needing to talk.

Later, as we paused for a short break at a turn in the trail, Glendalough's round tower, still miles away, came back into view like a distant whitish gray ship mast almost hidden from view among the branches of a still-leafless tree. This, no doubt, is what the ancient pilgrims had waited to see as they neared the end of their journey.

Again, I was struck by the "this-ness" of the landscape. Behind me lay endless miles of Wicklow mountain tops formed by seismic warping and magma extrusions and rounded off by ancient glaciers, and here—here—the monastic city comes into view between the branches of a leafless tree.

And the angel said, here, not there.

THE HOLY TRANSFORMS THE FAMILIAR

Some questions are dogged and will not go away. Is all land sacred? If Glendalough is a sacred place, is there another landscape that isn't? If the Creation is good and the landscape is spiritual, isn't all the earth sacred? Wendell Berry writes, "There are no unsacred places, only desecrated places."[6]

---

5. Mitchell and Ryan, *Reading the Irish Landscape*, 29.

6. Berry, *Given*.

Still, that seems too easy an answer although not necessarily an incorrect one. Haven't we all experienced a particular place that speaks to us more deeply than another, a place where the encounter with the past and the Holy is particularly intense? Even the rocks may cry out silently.

You may have found the hillside where the earth breathes.

Once, decades ago, on a late autumn hike at the Mines of Spain, Dianne and I wandered up through a hillside of straggly cedars, and stepped around a corner into a grove of birches, their white trunks and yellowing leaves etched sharply against a blue November sky.

Once, while camping with our oldest child yet a baby, his midnight cries sent us driving through the campground to lull him to sleep. The road took us down to the lake's boat landing, where our headlights shone out across the water into the thin mist that wisped above it like a breath. Into the misty cone of our headlights floated a canoe with a single paddler, and then, moments later, he passed back into the darkness. Our baby fell back asleep.

Once, our children now grown, Dianne and I hiked among Native American burial mounds on a Mississippi bluff, while far below us a sea of white gulls rode the wind crests above the river, rising and falling like waves of a shook linen blanket.

I call these moments Holy. I call these places Sacred.

What is the Holy, and what is the Sacred? Holy derives from an Old English word, *hālig*, meaning that which is whole and inviolate. It is a *quality*. The moment in the campground, mid-night, lakeside, the baby asleep, Dianne next to me in the car, the canoe passing before us—the moment as a unified Whole.

The Sacred, on the other hand, is a thing, an object, or—in this case—a place imbued with the Holy, immortalized, set apart. "Sacred" shares an etymological root with "sacrum," the bone at the base of the spine, the Holy Bone. An earthly thing made Holy. The place where the birches lit up with white trunks and yellow leaves against a blue sky. The valley where the gulls ride wind crests above the river.

The Holy transforms the familiar. The Holy makes the familiar sacred.

Are all places, then, sacred? Have all places been touched by the Holy? Am I speaking here of religion? As you wish.

§ § §

Sacred places may be far away and exotic, but so too may they be familiar. Either way, the common denominator is that the Sacred can't be hunted down and predictably found. It can only be revealed.

Theologian Beldon C. Lane describes both our longing to find the sacred grove as well as the Sacred's tendency to reveal itself where it will: "It is as if the human psyche were continually feeling along the surface of a great rock face, in search of the slightest fissure, a discontinuity that might afford entry beyond the rock to a numinal reality which both underlay and transcended the stone façade."[7] But sacred place "is not chosen, it chooses . . . Sacred place is ordinary place, ritually made extraordinary."[8]

For the Holy to transform the familiar place, it must also transform ordinary time and ordinary things. Celtic Christianity made holy the simplicity of daily life. Theologian Edward Sellner argues that the Celtic Christians' appreciation of ordinary life led them to value "the daily, the routine, the ordinary. They believed God is found not so much at the end of time when the reign of God *finally* comes, but *now,* where the reign is already being lived by God's faithful people."[9]

Even the continental monastic orders that would eventually piggyback on the Anglo-Norman invasion to replace Ireland's independent Celtic Christian abbeys were founded on such principles of simplicity and transformation of the familiar. A central tenet of the sixth-century Rule of Saint Benedict is that a monk "will regard all utensils and goods of the monastery as sacred vessels of the altar, aware that nothing is to be neglected."[10] I can think of no one who has expressed this as well as Brother Placid Zilka, a monk for more than sixty years at New Melleray Abbey, near Dubuque, Iowa, who explains, "Soil is sacred. St. Benedict tells in his Rule to treat the tools as vessels of the altar. Likewise are we to care for the soil. We stand on holy ground, so to speak."[11]

A similar attentiveness to the everyday world, the familiar, was called for by the vow of stability, which required Benedictine monks (and their offshoot, the Cistercian Trappists) to pledge to remain at the same monastery for the duration of their lives. In such circumstances, monastic men

7. Lane, *Landscapes of the Sacred*, 16

8. Lane, *Landscapes of the Sacred*, 15.

9. Sellner, *Wisdom of the Celtic Saints*, 25

10. *Rule of Saint Benedict*, 31:10-11.

11. Zilka, Personal Interview.

and women must be attentive to the sacred where they are in everyday life and everyday surroundings, rather than seeking it elsewhere.

Father Columban Heaney, a Trappist monk for more than sixty years at Ireland's Mount Melleray Abbey, parent monastery to New Melleray, extolls the necessity of monks finding the spiritual within the details of everyday life: "There's a peace, quietness, stillness here. People don't find God [in modern society] because there are too many distractions. That's why people come here for a day, a week, two weeks. You either find God in monastic life or you leave again."[12]

Father Jonah Wharf of New Melleray Abbey points out the Trappist tradition of encountering the Holy in everyday work: "In Cistercian monasticism we live by 'Ora et labora,' pray and work. The Trappist tradition began with the desire to return to manual labor, to get back to a simple life of prayer and work. Trappists traditionally farmed, and the development of the interior life is related to farming in that one has to learn to be dependent on what one has no control over, such as blight and drought. We develop a virtue of trust."[13]

The familiar, in such cases, is everyday work, everyday routines, everyday places, made sacred by the presence of the Holy. It is dirt under the fingernails, transformed. Eric Anglada, who along with his wife Brenna, tends St. Isadore Catholic Worker farm in rural southwest Wisconsin, puts it this way:

> The work with which I have been engaged over much of the past eight years on the farm [St. Isadore, and before that, New Hope Catholic Worker Farm] is the quotidian work of subsistence, of supporting the home: splitting firewood with an ax, gardening with hand tools, tending chickens and cows, washing clothes, cooking with wood heat and cleaning the almost endless mountain of dishes a kitchen full of home-grown ingredients will inevitably produce . . . It is work of deep spiritual value.[14]

Liamy Mac Nally, an Irish Catholic priest who now works as a journalist in western Ireland, regrets the Church's loss of such a gritty connection with the earth: "The Roman Church has lost the primal touch of the early Church." Mac Nally argues that many of the actions of the Catholic Mass have their roots in primal touch, but the touch has been lost and only the

12. Heaney, Personal Interview.

13. Wharf, Personal Interview.

14. Anglada, "Homecoming," 30.

actions retained. When the priest washes his hands before the Offertory, saying "Lord, wash away my iniquities and cleanse me from my sins," the "cleansing" originated because the offering was once hen's eggs, dairy products, and homemade products brought in by the people instead of money. The priest would receive them, then wash his hands before consecrating the bread and wine. The words and actions are still present in the Mass today, but they are no longer rooted in earthy contact. "The Catholic Church ought to be a church where you get your hands dirty," Mac Nally laments.[15]

For many, experiencing the Holy and coming into contact with sacred place has burst from traditional confines and found new expressions. Sister Bernadette Flanagan of Dublin explains that alongside the implosion of institutional religion in Ireland, there has been a simultaneous return to nature-based Shamanism and Druidism.[16] Aran Islands Celtic monk Dara Molloy sees the modern movements of sustainability and local foods as having a spiritual dimension: "Growing your own food or supporting local growers helps get you back into a sense of place, to associate with the seasons and traditions of that place."[17] Such intimacy with the landscape leads to encounter with the loca sacra.

The encounter with the Holy need not be religious, nor the sacred grove be a monastic ruin. A sense of wonder, awe, and amazement will define the spiritual moment for some.

The Holy is not necessarily found in the most stunningly beautiful landscapes. Instead, attentiveness to the world can help us find the Holy where we least expect it. Finding the Holy in turn transforms the landscape into a sacred place. Philip Sheldrake, in *Spaces for the Sacred*, reminds us that theologian Karl Rahner had called grace God's "inspirit-ing" of the world. There is, says Sheldrake, a "mysticism of everyday life in the world of ordinary places."[18]

There is a grove of birch among the rough cedars. A canoe floating in the mist through the car headlights. A bluff above the river where the gulls lift and lilt on the crests of the wind.

There is the hill where the earth breathes.

These are the Thin Places, where the tactile this-ness of the earth becomes holy.

15. Mac Nally, Personal Interview.

16. Flanagan, Personal Interview.

17. Molloy, Personal Interview.

18. Sheldrake,. *Spaces for the Sacred*, 145.

To find them, says, Father Frank Fahey of Ballintubber Abbey in County Mayo, "You have to develop an 'inner eye' to grasp the truth about a place as the mystics did." [19]

THE MINES OF SPAIN

I first came upon them several years ago in the dead of winter. Up a steep, snowy climb adjacent to an abandoned quarry, past the 150-year-old oaks, down and back up the other side of a sharply etched ravine, I'd stumbled onto one, then a few, then dozens and hundreds of shallow pits strewn about the woods on a bluff overlooking the Mississippi River at the Mines of Spain. Judging by the lack of footprints in the snow, no one had been here lately.

It looked like a bomb crater field. When I realized that before me lay the remnant lead mine diggings of the very first Euro-American settlers, this patch of regrown forest transformed before my eyes.

§ § §

The Mines of Spain is a 1,400-acre state-owned preserve along the Mississippi River just south of the city of Dubuque. The French-Canadian Julien Dubuque was given exclusive permission by the Meskwaki tribe and their chief Peosta in 1788 to mine lead along twenty-one miles of Mississippi shoreline and nine miles inland. He was the first permanent white settler in what was to become the state of Iowa. But Dubuque double-protected his claim a decade later when he petitioned the Spanish government in Louisiana—which then controlled all of the land west of the Mississippi—to mine the area he proposed to call, in a politically astute manner, the Mines of Spain. His request was granted in 1797.

Dubuque must have made a little life for himself there in the Catfish Creek valley, extracting 20,000-30,000 pounds of lead a year, which he transported to St. Louis by canoe. Upon his death in 1810, his estate included "furnishings and dishes of some value" he'd brought back with him or had delivered, undoubtedly at some expense, from St. Louis. In a largely illiterate countryside, his possessions also included fifty-eight books, among them works of political philosophy and encyclopedias of art.

---

19. Fahey, Personal Interview.

The inventory of his possessions, however, was conducted to pay off his debts to St. Louis financiers.[20]

The Meskwaki lived intermittently at the mouth of Catfish Creek, but finally abandoned the village in 1830, due to Lakota raids. Euro-American miners from across the Illinois shore rushed in to fill the void. Lucius Langworthy, one of the miners, described the deserted, mournful village they found:

> A large [Meskwaki] village was then standing at the mouth of Catfish Creek. About seventy buildings were constructed with poles, and the bark of trees remained to tell of those who had so recently inhabited them. Their Council House, though rude, was ample in its dimensions, and contained a great many furnaces, in which kettles had been placed, to prepare the feasts of peace or war . . . On the inner surface of the bark there were paintings done with considerable artistic skill, representing the buffalo, elk, bear, panther, and other animals of the chase; also their wild sports on the prairie, and even their feats in war.[21]

The miners then burned the village.

The U.S. military drove the miners away a few months later, as the western shore of the Mississippi was not yet open to American settlement. When the Meskwaki were forced to cede the area in the aftermath of the 1832 Black Hawk War, the miners biding time across the river rushed in again, this time for good.

The earliest miners chipped out veins of lead that erupted from cliff exposures and dug shallow pits where lead lay just below the bedrock. These were the surface diggings I had chanced upon in the woods above the river.

Later mines were more elaborate. Miners sunk vertical shafts up to forty feet deep, carved out horizontal veins and reinforced them with timber, laid down cart track for raw ore, and carried out the wealth of the land. By 1852 the miners were hauling 26 million pounds of lead a year from the hills, producing 90 percent of the country's supply.

The nearby Riprow Valley and the bluffs above the Mississippi teemed with immigrant miners, smelters, and, soon enough, the Catfish Stream Sawmill. The woods disappeared day by day as miners felled timber for ore-smelting, for the newly burgeoning railroad's appetite, and for the new town taking shape to the north.

20. Auge, "The Life and Times of Julien Dubuque," 11-12.

21. Wilkie, *Dubuque on the Mississippi*, 125.

Lead mining peaked in the 1850s, then dwindled over the next two decades. By the late 1870s it had largely ceased. The mine pits I had come upon in the snow had lain abandoned for 150 years, and the woods grown back among them were precisely the age of the oldest, most massive oaks I'd stopped to admire.

This was no longer a familiar woods, but the familiar made Holy by its lingering story.

§ § §

My sister passed away a few years ago. So the past was on my mind as I took a break from it all and headed to the Mines of Spain to snowshoe in late February, shortly after her death. After a steep climb I emerged onto a hog-back, the term for a narrow ridge with steeply sloping or cliff-faced edges.

In the crest of the next hill over, I thought I'd spied a lead mine pit. Lead mines are distinguishable from sinkholes—another frequent feature of this limestone landscape—by the little lip of rock and soil surrounding the hole, dug up and tossed from the pit by the miners. But when I next saw a line of three small swells of earth rising up from the forest floor, I knew them to be Hopewellian burial mounds dating from 750 to 2,500 years old. The pit alongside them, I realized, was no lead mine at all, but an old violation of the grave.

This was no longer *any* woods, but the familiar made Holy by fracture.

§ § §

When I first came upon the field of lead mine pits, I paused and looked about. I was alone in the woods in a snow mottled by late afternoon sunlight splintering down through the branches of the overhead canopy. And suddenly the woods began to fill with Irish immigrant miners chipping away here and there at subsurface rocks, yelling to each other, a laugh, then a curse, two men pausing on a spill pile eating horrid lunches and swigging from beer growlers lugged up from the hollow. A cart wrenches into movement, piled with rock headed to the lead smelter.

On the next hill over, the woods fills with Hopewellian Indians hauling baskets of sacred soil up from the river valley to inter the dead in burial mounds. And when they fade from the landscape a white man with a shovel unearths some bones from one of the mounds and squirrels away his loot in a sack.

Then it is quiet again and I am alone.

These woods are not so different from the next hill over, except for the miners, except for the violated graves, except for the mountain behind the mountain.

For the Holy transforms the familiar and makes of it a sacred place.

THE PORTAL

After Julien Dubuque's death in 1810, the Meskwaki buried him on the blufftop above the Mississippi River, his grave marked with a small cabin-like structure which eventually decayed. In 1897 the local townsfolk unearthed his bones, photographed them, and duly reburied them beneath a twenty-five-foot-tall medieval-style monument with castlements atop.

A male Indian's bones, believed to be Chief Peosta's, and a female Indian's, possibly Dubuque's wife of lore, the chief's daughter Potosa, were likewise found on the spot during the 1897 excavation. These were carted off to a garish local museum display, until they were more respectfully buried near (but separate from) Julien Dubuque eighty years later.

The Spring equinox sunrise lights up the interior of Dubuque's grave. Several minutes later, as the sun climbs higher in the sky, it finally lights up Peosta's grave as well. These are old, old lands, inhabited as long as the hills of Ireland, but forgotten in the midst of an American genocide. The suppressed memory, sun-warmed, begins to stir.

Chapter 4

Bealtaine: Time is Cyclical And Elastic in the Thin Places

BEALTAINE, MAY 1

By May 1, the Celtic feast of Bealtaine [BE-AHL-tin-eh], the Driftless Land is knee-deep in spring and rushing giddily toward summer. Back at my house, the grass has turned a sharp green that could slice a May blue sky. The woods lag slightly behind. The oak canopy is mint-shaded in the early stages of budding.

Daylight is stretching exponentially. At the Julien Dubuque Monument on Bealtaine, the sky begins to lighten about 5:30 a.m., with sunrise at 5:57 Central Daylight Time, an hour earlier than on the equinox just six weeks ago.

And bird chatter, absent from my year of Celtic sunrises thus far, ushers in the dawn.

There on the horizon—the red fire of sunrise!

§ § §

In Celtic Ireland, Bealtaine was one of the four quarter festivals, the name meaning "bright fire." Bealtaine celebrated the awakening of the land, the true spring, a celebration of life and fertility.

On Bealtaine Eve, Druid priests lit twin fires at the "center" of Ireland, at Uisneach in County Meath, to celebrate the "eyes of the earth goddess

63

Eriu opening to the new season."[1] When Druid priests at the sacred Hill of Tara spotted the Uisneach bonfires in the distance, they in turn lit twin fires at Tara as well, and in progression, like a wave pushing out from the center, Bealtaine bonfires lit up across the Irish countryside.

Bealtaine rituals also involved domestic life. At Bealtaine, everyone from kings to cottagers doused their hearth fires and relit them from the community blaze. Early May was also the time to lead cattle from winter shelter to summer pastures. Farmers started the season by marching their cattle around or between the Bealtaine bonfires. Dancers leapt across the fires, signaling that the season had crossed over into early summer.

Bealtaine rituals were said to enhance sexual allure and assure fertility. Maidens rolled in the Bealtaine dew or spread it across their faces to increase attractiveness, young couples spent the prior night together in the hills, ostensibly gathering mayflowers for the Bealtaine celebration, and Maypole dances themselves evoked erotic imagery. Colonial British Puritans outlawed Bealtaine rituals in 1644, but the festival persisted in Ireland.[2]

At Bealtaine, the boundaries between the human and the otherworld dissolved in the mystical Thin Places. In *The Music of What Happens*, John O'Ríordáin explains, "At these times in particular . . . the fairy dwellings were open, thus permitting humans to enter and the Tuatha De Danann [the fabled fairy people of Ireland] to emerge."[3] But whereas Samhain's festival of the dead brought trouble-making, Bealtaine's spirits and fairies simply sought contact with the human world. Time at Bealtaine was all-time, with the gods and the dead and the fairies and the living all afoot.

In Patrick mythology, St. Patrick used the Bealtaine bonfire ritual to one-up the Druids in contention for Irish souls. One legend tells of Patrick circumventing the pagan ritual by lighting his own bonfire ahead of the Druids at nearby Slane Hill. When Druids rushed to Slane in anger, Patrick preached to and converted them, transforming the Bealtaine ritual into an Easter celebration. He is said to have boasted, "In this hour all paganism in Ireland has been destroyed."[4]

Over time, Bealtaine morphed in one direction into May Day, or Mary's Day, and in another into secular bonfire-themed local folk festivals

1. Monaghan, *The Red-Haired Girl from the Bog*, 175
2. Monaghan, *The Encyclopedia of Celtic Mythology and Folklore*, 42.
3. O'Ríordáin, *The Music of What Happens*, 38.
4. Monaghan, *The Red-Haired Girl from the Bog*, 174.

of music, art, and dance, including a huge annual festival still held at Uisneach. That said, Bealtaine is perhaps the least observed and least known of the four Celtic festivals today, although a vestige remains in the Irish secular holiday observed on the first Monday of May, known simply as the May Bank Holiday.

Neither the Irish nor my Driftless neighbors believe in Bealtaine fairies anymore. But a holiday here and a feast day there stretches the hours and the days that otherwise hurtle forward. The widening arc of the sun as we pass from another winter reminds us we've been this way before.

THE BURREN

I arrive in the Burren on a Sunday afternoon in Spring, just a few weeks before Bealtaine will begin to stretch the summer sun, to join in on a hike led by Tony Kirby, a hillwalking guide who, more than a decade ago, left the stability of a public sector job in Dublin for life in the Burren, one of Ireland's most noteworthy Thin Places.[5] In the Burren, nothing is quite as it seems. Amid the bleak moonscape of exposed bedrock lies Ireland's richest array of wildflowers and some of its most productive agricultural land. What appears to be a dry, desert landscape is in fact visited by frequent rains that drain quickly into the cavernous limestone. Even the small lakes and ponds, called turloughs, visible now in Spring, are deceptive: when the water table drops in summer, the lakes will mysteriously disappear.

The Burren is a 200-square-mile region in County Clare, Ireland, famous for endless stretches of flat, rectangular, grey limestone surface bedrock slabs called "pavement," reaching to the horizon in all directions, tumbling into ravines and scaling the low-lying mountains. Its name, appropriately, derives from an Irish word, "Boíreann," meaning "a rocky place."

"Not enough water to drown a man, not enough wood to hang him, and not enough soil to bury him" claimed a henchman of Oliver Cromwell in the 1650s, describing the Burren region of western Ireland as British troops scoured the land, searching for rebels to the Crown.

Lesser known is the rest of the Cromwellian's observation: "And yet their cattle are very fat; for the grass growing in turfs of earth . . . that lie between the rocks, which are of limestone, is very sweet and nourishing."

5. Kirby, Personal Interview. Kirby is founder of Heart of Burren Walks.

Barren and bleak, bustling with life, the Burren is a place of contradictions. From the thin crevices (called grikes) between the slabs (called clints), flowers such as the spring gentian are hardy enough to withstand the cool, wet, wind-beaten winters. They thrive on the intense sunlight reflected off the limestone pavement that mimics the light intensity of alpine ice and snow.

On the other hand, a large assortment of Mediterranean orchids also grace the Burren. They find just enough warmth amid the limestone pavements that absorb and reradiate sun's heat. Mediterranean flowers survive because the Burren rarely freezes, warmed by the Atlantic Gulf Stream that bathes Ireland's west coast.

In my early spring visit to the Burren, the cobalt-blue spring gentian is making its appearance alongside the endless gray slabs. Life amid the rocks is poising to burst.

Six of us head out across the Burren with Tony in the lead: a young couple from Sligo, a father and daughter visiting from Limerick, a university student from Tennessee studying abroad in Dublin, and myself. The Irish hillwalkers flit easily across the rocky landscape behind Tony as if the grikes have magically disappeared, while the American student and I balance each footstep among the perilous rocks with arms outstretched like squirrel tails.

In the Burren, all time is present time. The surface limestone was formed at sea bottom in tropical regions 350 million years ago. Tony points out some coral fossils in the upland limestone: the tiny cone-shaped stony remnants look like they are still undulating in shallow salt waters.

On the Burren, it seems as if the glaciers have just retreated. The rugged landscape took its present shape during the last ice age, ending twelve thousand years ago. The glacial ice, a half-mile thick over Ireland, flowed slowly but resolutely. The relentless ice scraped soil away from the uplands and shunted it into the crevices between the blocks of exposed surface limestone. Meanwhile, the glaciers deposited sands, clays, and gravels in the valleys, forming fertile tear-drop shaped hills, called drumlins. Elsewhere in the Burren lie glacial erratics, boulders carried by the glaciers and dropped randomly across the expanse. On the drive to our hiking ground, we pass a field of erratics known as the Playground of the Gods, where car-sized boulders lie scattered like gigantic toys left behind just yesterday when the gods disappeared as quietly as turloughs in summer.

Neolithic farmers depleted much of the Burren's remaining topsoil through erosional farming practices five thousand years ago, a process that author Tim Robinson called "agri-vandalism." They cleared forests from the highlands because their stone tools could cut through the upland ash and hazel trees more easily than through the dense lowland oaks. When the climate turned wetter, windier, and warmer, the thin upland soil washed away, exposing today's Burren limestone pavement expanse. Thousands of years of weathering have continued the process.

Shadows of Neolithic civilization still abound. Nearly a hundred pre-historic tombs dot the Burren landscape. These tombs typically consist of two or three 6-8 foot tall limestone slab-walls set vertically, supporting a roof slab, giving the appearance of a tottering house of cards, although they have remained stable through five thousand years of weathering.

If early farmers destroyed their own nest, later farmers turned the landscape to their advantage. The Burren owes its modern look to cattle grazing. The lush grasses that grow in pockets and clumps between the stony slabs nourished the cattle that Celtic kings—and later Norman, British, and finally Irish landowners—boasted as the essence of Irish wealth. In turn, cattle kept the underbrush trimmed. Left unchecked, in time the underbrush would have covered the rocky expanse. As Tony says, "The custodians of the uplands are the cows."

The Burren is popular with tourists although much of its traffic is headed along the better roads to the Cliffs of Moher, one of Ireland's most-visited attractions. The curious will stop to examine the Poulnabrone portal tomb. For a taste and smell of the old ways, they will drop in on the peat-warmed pubs of nearby Doolin and Lisdoonvarna for a pint of Guinness and a bowl of Irish stew, staking out a nook amid meandering rooms. The evenings are filled with traditional music.

But a few days after my hike with Tony, I am headed off the tourist path, driving on one-lane roads where I must back up one hundred feet to let a local farmer's tractor, the day's only traffic, slip past me. Here I find a seldom-visited Neolithic wedge tomb and a Columbkille-founded monastic ruin hidden away from the touring buses, guarded only by the upland sheep and cattle. I am alone on a rocky, mountainous back road—not even any local farmers in sight—and it feels like I could be swallowed into the landscape. I am in a Thin Place.

It's all there at once, intermingled, these shallow sea deposits, glacial carvings, Neolithic tombs, medieval ruins, and a backroad farmer's tractor. An ever-present now.

TIME IS CYCLICAL AND ELASTIC IN THE THIN PLACES

On Bealtaine Eve I drive up to Ballybofen, County Donegal, with the intent of staying overnight and arriving at the Beltany Stone Circle before the break of dawn. The stone circle, one of the largest in Ireland, takes its name from the Bealtaine feast and offers a May 1 sunrise alignment above one of the key stones.

The drive to Ballybofen turns out to be one of the easiest of my stay in western Ireland—all relatively wide and straight National roads. Arriving in the early afternoon without having once been lost, I decide to locate the stone circle in daylight so I can find it more easily tomorrow morning before dawn.

The day's easy drive, however, ends in a tangle of unmarked, narrow country roads when I exit the N15 and zigzag upward toward the stone circle. When Google Maps leads me to a muddy turnaround at the end of a paved road, I realize that I will be making no such venture into the dark in the morning. A Bealtaine Eve's daylight visit to the Beltany stone circle will suffice just fine, thank you. Besides, the forecast is for clouds and rain in the morning.

I finally spy a road sign pointing in the direction of the stone circle—it is, after all, a National Heritage site, remote and unvisited as it may be. And then, after an absence of road markings for the next few intersections, I see another sign. When I pull up to the small, off-road parking spot, one other car is present, belonging to a man and his two young daughters who are descending the entrance lane as I walk in.

A few drops of cold rain pelt down as I emerge from the lane and step out into the pasture at the promontory hill where the stone circle lies.

I am not prepared for what I see in the midst of the sheep pastures. I have never seen such a large stone circle, with sixty-four stones completing the ring. The thin-slabbed stones jut from the raised interior at jagged angles like shark teeth, like centuries-old tombstones. A triangular stone dimpled with what archaeologists call "cup holes" marks where the rising Bealtaine sun would clear the tree line, touch the tip of the stone, and light the circle's interior.

I eat my lunch in the center of the circle: ham, cheese, an apple, perhaps not that much different from a Bronze Age diet. Back east at Uisneach a massive, noisy folk fest would now be getting underway, but I prefer my

Bealtaine this way, alone in a stone circle on a promontory hill surrounded by a sheep pasture.

The day stretches out before me, and I grab it like an apple. I examine the jagged stones from outside the circle and then from the inside. I lie on my stomach before the triangular alignment stone, imagining the sunrise clearing the trees to the east and balancing precariously and momentarily on the stone's apex. I hang out for an hour or more—sitting, wandering, wondering. No one else comes visiting.

I'd like to tell you that I had a shamanistic vision of Celtic Druids preparing the evening's bonfire. But I'm not prone to exaggeration. My only claim is that in certain places and at certain times all time feels present. I felt this in the Beltany stone circle.

Time, as we usually experience it, is linear and one-directional. Yesterday has disappeared into a turlough hole and cannot be relived. The present suns itself briefly on the limestone pavement and evaporates in a wavering heat. The future brews out on the Atlantic and all too soon will be whipping the coast.

This linearity is time as we understand it, but not necessarily time as it actually exists or as it is always perceived. Indigenous peoples—including Celtic and Native American—often view time differently, as cyclical and elastic.

In cyclical time, the repetitions of nature and communal life outweigh the perception of time's forward march. The days repeat in endless fashion, the seasons repeat, the arc of life repeats. Forward-moving time is more like a rolling hoop than a vector-pathed arrow. As the hoop rolls forward, any point on the circle cycles endlessly from top to bottom to top again. The individual moves through youth, adulthood, and old age, but always, communally, there are infants cooing, adolescents testing limits, parents providing, and elderly imparting wisdom until age and infirmity again render them needy.

Time for indigenous cultures may be elastic as well. The tick-tock regularity of the invented clock gives way to time that expands and contracts as the lived moment intensifies or recedes. Many of us experience this, but in a negative way: Time flies when you're having fun.

Elastic time pervades the Celtic story of Tír na nÓg, a mythical island west of Ireland occupied by faeries descended from the Tuatha dé Danann. In Tír na nÓg, all time is present time. It is not a succession of todays lined up on into the future, but a single today, always. If time passes at all, it passes slowly.

Humans in Celtic mythology occasionally visit Tír na nÓg, either having sailed upon it by accident or having been lured there by a lovelorn fairy, as in the story of the poet Oisin. [6] When Niamh of the Golden Hair, the fairy daughter of the king of Tír na nÓg, visits the humans of Ireland and falls in love with the young Oisin, she entices him to return with her to the mystical island. There, Oisin later recounts, "I lived in the Land of Youth more than three hundred years; but it appeared to me that only three years had passed since the day I parted from my friends."

When Oisin eventually becomes homesick, Niamh grants him a temporary return but warns him not to dismount from his white steed lest he touch the ground and instantly age and die. Finding that his parents and friends have long since passed away, Oisin wanders about Ireland on his horse. At Glenasmole, seven miles south of Dublin, he encounters a group of Irishmen laboring to save a man from a crushing stone slab that has fallen on him. Ossian, though human, is a member of the now-vanished giant race, the Fiana, and the desperate crowd cries out for the giant's help. Ossian comes to their aid and heaves the rock while seated on his horse, but the movement is jarring and he is flung from his horse to the earth where he instantly becomes "a poor, withered old man, blind and wrinkled and feeble." In Tír na nÓg, time had stretched indefinitely for Ossian but came crashing down around him when he set foot again on solid ground.

In the Thin Places, the past occurs alongside the present, just slightly removed behind the permeable veil. All souls of that place are present at once. In his essay, "Grave," Robert MacFarlane discusses the coexistence of the living and the dead in one such locale: "The Burren, it seemed that sunlit afternoon, also possessed these different orders of existence, moving in relation to one another. At certain times and in certain places . . . one could see through the present land, the land of the living, backwards into another time, to a ghost landscape, the land of the dead." [7]

Early Celtic Christians retained this cyclical, elastic view of time held by their ancestors. Author Edward Sellner explains: "The Celts' perception was that there is a fullness *now* to all of time . . . For them, the present

6. The story of Oisin is taken from Joyce, *Old Celtic Romances*, 385-400.

7. MacFarlane, *The Wild Places*, 169

contains within itself both past events, which continue to live on, as well as the seeds of future events waiting to be born."[8]

This Celtic view put Irish Christians at odds with the continental Church which only perceived the present forever receding into the past along a linear path pointed inexorably toward a future heaven or hell.

In the Americas, Native American culture expresses an interconnection of time, story and place not unlike the Celts'. According to Jim Bear Jacobs, a Mohican pastor of the Twin-Cities-based Church of All Nations:

> In the western mindset of linear thinking, time is perceived as moving in straight-line fashion. History in the West exists in time, so our stories exist in time, which creates a distance from and limits access to stories. For Natives, stories are not chronologically linked but are connected to places. When we visit the places where certain events occurred, we feel the presence of story in that space.[9]

In such a framework, the past remains alive in present places.

Chloris Lowe of the Ho-Chunk Nation links the continuity of the past to landscapes associated with a person's spirit. Speaking of Native American burial mounds, Lowe explains, "If the spirits of ancestors are in the mounds and the overall landscape, some of that life-spirit is taken up in the trees and grasses that grow from the soil where people once lived."[10] The present landscape, in this sense, keeps the past alive.

Burren native and author John O'Donohue offers the following prescription for living in the present, in presence: "We cannot consider God in any chronological time frame. The calendar is no guide to the divine ground. God is not subject to the linearity of human time. Everything in God subsists in the most radical nowness. God is Nowness."[11]

§ § §

On Bealtaine Eve's day at the Beltany stone circle in County Mayo, Ireland, the afternoon spreads out before me like spring time's lengthening daylight.

---

8. Sellner, *Wisdom of the Celtic Saints*, 24.

9. Jacobs, Telephone Interview.

10. Lowe, Personal Interview.

11. O'Donohue, *The Four Elements*, 11-12.

When the sky clouds over above the circle and a drizzling rain begins falling again, I zip up my jacket, grab my backpack, and leave the circle as the veil seals shut.

KICKAPOO VALLEY RESERVE

It was another year's April, nearing Bealtaine, when I first visited the Kickapoo Valley Reserve in southwest Wisconsin. The ground was spongy with recent rains and snowmelt. The Kickapoo River swelled and threatened its banks.

At the Reserve, I followed an asphalt lane, known as Old Highway 131, that wound through the valley floor. At that time, the road was a bit worn, with grass encroaching on its edges and its pavement crumbling in occasional patches. But with the new Highway 131 hugging the upland ridge, the old road had now become a multi-use recreation trail through the 8,600-acre reserve.

I followed Old 131 downstream and crossed a handsome covered bridge. And suddenly out of the late afternoon's gray mist arose before me a 150-foot tall earthen wall slung halfway across the valley floor, stopping short of the skittish river. I thought I'd stumbled into a Thin Place.

§ § §

The Kickapoo meanders more than a hundred river miles in a 66-mile as-the-crow-flies stretch of southwest Wisconsin, draining a half-million acres aided by 140 watershed tributaries. It is prone to flooding. After major floods ravaged the downstream towns of La Farge, Viola, Readstown, and Soldiers Grove at least five times in three decades, in 1969 the federal government's Army Corps of Engineers began buying up 149 farms with plans to build a 1780-acre lake for the twin purposes of flood control and water recreation. By 1975 the 110-foot grey, concrete drain tower was in place and an earthen dam had been built halfway across the valley. Old 131 appeared destined to the watery floor of the future lake.

But the plan to dam the Kickapoo didn't hold water.

The 1970 National Environmental Policy Act required an environmental impact study at the site prior to its completion. The study revealed numerous rare and endangered plant and animal species that would be destroyed by the proposed lake, such as northern monkshood, a blue springtime wildflower shaped, of course, like the hood of a monk's cowl. It is a rare relict wildflower left over from the ice age and found only in a few cool-climate corners of the state. Rare wood turtles and box turtles, along with red-shouldered hawks and bald eagles, would suffer habitat loss as well.

Meanwhile, archaeological studies revealed Native American thunderbird petroglyphs, village campsite artifacts, and rock shelters where ancient peoples overwintered as far back as 1500 BC. "In the early seventies it was just accepted that these sites would be destroyed by damming the river," says Kickapoo Valley Reserve Executive Director Marcy West.[12]

The final hole in the plans was a University of Wisconsin follow-up study that indicated additional geological challenges that could undermine the reservoir, recreational boating, and overall flood control efforts.

By this point $18 million had already been spent on the project, about half of the original anticipated cost. Even if the Corps received permission to flood the valley despite its endangered species and Native American archaeological sites, project redesigns now meant that $51 million (not $20 million) would be required to complete the work.

So in 1975 the Corps of Engineers pulled the plug.

The land then sat in limbo for the next twenty years while the nearby community seethed. Many of the 149 former landowners had been reluctant sellers and now saw the project abandoned. Other locals who had been eager for flood control and a good fishing lake now saw only a government boondoggle. Meanwhile, the 8,500 acres that had been removed from community tax rolls left schools and local governments short of funds.

By the early 1990s state and local officials had had enough. For a variety of reasons the land could no longer be returned to the original owners, so an advisory committee convened and proposed turning the property into a nature reserve hosting low-impact tourism and educational programs. Twelve hundred acres were returned to the Ho-Chunk tribe, the most recent Native American inhabitants of the area and who still have a sizeable presence in the region.

§ § §

Something keeps circling me back to the Kickapoo Valley Reserve. It's hard to put my finger on it. The Driftless Land is rich in tributaries to the Mississippi River, but something about the meandering Kickapoo and its steep sandstone walls repeatedly lures me to make the two-hour drive from

---

12. West, Personal Interview.

my home. Bluffs, rock towers, and deep ravines are frequent throughout the Driftless, but the wooded and rugged Kickapoo hills seem even more steeped in these. I could find marshy wetlands filled with cattails and red-wing blackbirds closer to home, but the ponds along Old 131 come instantly to mind.

Perhaps what draws me is the close call of the Kickapoo valley to ruin. Hiking along Old 131, I am aware all at once of the past, the present, and at least one version of a future that never unfolded.

§ § §

The Ho-Chunk claim an ancestry linking them back to the mound-builders of the Upper Mississippi Valley and even more deeply to the earliest peoples who migrated into the Driftless region near the end of the glacial period. Archaeological evidence increasingly bears out the longtime tribal belief.

The Ho-Chunk were likewise the last Native American tribe to occupy the Kickapoo Valley. Events leading to their forced displacement devolved over several decades in the early nineteenth century through a series of ignored and abused treaties. An 1816 treaty between the U.S. government and the Ho-Chunk (then commonly known as the Winnebago) promised to set boundaries among tribes and protect Indian lands from incursions by white settlers. These promises went largely ignored by the 1820s when lead mining prospects became irresistible in the region.

And even though the Ho-Chunk Nation was not involved in the Black Hawk War, after the conflict concluded with the defeat of Black Hawk, the massacre of his followers, and their removal from lands east of the Mississippi River, the U.S. government seized the moment to also remove the Ho-Chunk from southwest Wisconsin. An 1837 treaty, misunderstood and negotiated with unauthorized tribe members, forced the Ho-Chunk to relocate to a buffer zone on the west banks of the Mississippi, planting them like human shields between the Sauk and Sioux, who were each other's arch-rivals in the battle for dwindling lands.

Many of the Ho-Chunk refused to leave and simply dispersed into the Wisconsin landscape. When the government next forced the remaining Ho-Chunk even further west, to Minnesota, South Dakota, and finally to Omaha, Nebraska, some of the Ho-Chunk slipped into their canoes on the Missouri River, paddled downstream and then circled back up the Mississippi to return to their home landscape in southwestern Wisconsin.[13]

13. Indian Country Wisconsin.

When the citizens' advisory committee proposed turning the Kickapoo Valley into a nature reserve with low-impact tourism, the Ho-Chunk helped mollify former landowners who still felt burnt that their lands had been taken against their will and the reservoir never built. Perhaps like no one else, the Ho-Chunk could evoke in the former landowners a degree of shared history of wrested homelands. In some sense, time had circled back on itself.

In 1996, the Kickapoo Reserve Management Board hired Marcy West as its Executive Director. West's challenge was to find the right balance between habitat preservation and outdoor activity. Kids' activities like "Space Camp" and "Jeepers Creepers" adorn the summer calendar, while adults join in on a summer solstice stargaze or guided hikes. Nearly 20,000 visitors came to the Reserve in 2016, up from 15,000 just a few short years ago. West attributes the rising numbers, in part, to growing interest in the Driftless Land.

Amid such success, West's balancing task is to protect the Reserve's natural habitat. Each spring, West and her staff burn about fifty to seventy-five acres of their 200-acre prairie on a rotated schedule as part of prairie restoration and maintenance. In spring 2016 the Reserve staff also conducted their first-ever hardwood timber harvest from their 4,000-acre forest. "Selective harvest improves the health of the stand to create a better mix of oak and hardwoods," West explains.

West can tell you about the numerical and programmatic successes of the Kickapoo Valley Reserve. But she can also tell you about its healing and soothing effects, for herself and for others. When I talked with her one recent afternoon, we sat on a deck in the sun outside the Visitor Center as she explained that she likes to canoe the Kickapoo in the early spring and late fall best among the seasons, because "I can get on the river alone. Just last week I was canoeing on the river alone and saw an eagle perched on a branch fifteen feet away who just watched me float on by."

Perhaps the creation of a nature reserve rather than an artificial lake offered more healing for those who, over the generations, have loved this valley and then had it taken from them. The call of bullfrogs and honking geese in the wetlands might, in the long run, bring about more peace than the whining of motor boats. West links the Ho-Chunk and twentieth-century landowners' experiences, saying, "What the people who lived here had to go through breaks your heart. But I love to see them come back and comment that the Reserve is probably the best result."

The Kickapoo River and its cultural milieu have altered West's world-view and her view of time: "I have been influenced by Ho-Chunk board members thinking seven generations out," West says, explaining the practice of considering how today's actions will affect the distant future. Present decisions in such a framework are interconnected with the past and future.

There is a Bealtaine here, a fresh start on life after a bitter cold winter.

§ § §

Before I leave the Reserve, West recommends that I use the rest of my afternoon to climb to Blackhawk Rock, a sandstone tower overlooking the Kickapoo Valley. And so I take her advice.

The trail leading up to Black Hawk Rock winds around the base of the tower, circling upward, clockwise, till it arrives at a hogback spine that gradually narrows to a couple of feet in width, with sharp drop-offs on either side. The hogback spine descends slightly to the cliff face.

The wind this day is strong and steady—more than I'm comfortable with at the top of the cliff outcrop. I remove my ballcap to keep it from blowing off into the valley. The view from here oversees miles of Driftless hills. Old 131 barely peeks through in the valley alongside small slices of the Kickapoo River.

All time is present in this Thin Place. This, too, has been a rock of ages, a meaningful place for people across the centuries. The Ho-Chunk held rite-of-passage rituals on this rock outcrop. Back at the Visitors Center old photos show pioneers wedging themselves into the crevasses of the rock tower base, having chosen this place for a rare day away from the fields. And modern rituals continue, says West, smiling about a man who recently proposed to his girlfriend atop Blackhawk Rock.

And so I have wedged myself into the rock tower's past as well. But I try to hold this place lightly, knowing that my true home lies two hours south, and the valley is already crowded with souls who loved this land and lost it.

But if a turbulent past swirls about this place in the low clouds forming to the west, the present and future are, for the moment at least, bonded together by the simple fact that no dam is going to swallow up the valley.

I'd like to lose my own sense of time and self, and sit here, unthinking, for as long as it takes for all thought to dissolve and disappear between the cracks in the rock. But time back home is still on its arrow. I have too much German-heritage upbringing in me: I have set a time limit so I can get back down on the trail, back on the road, back home to Dubuque for the evening's obligations.

And so as I hike back down the trail and take one last look behind me to where the sun has filtered through the forest canopy, Blackhawk Rock slowly dissolves into the dappled afternoon.

THE PORTAL

Henry David Thoreau taught me about the relationship between rivers and time when he wrote that time's "thin current slides away, but eternity remains." [14] Like time itself, water flows, but the river remains.

For if the Mississippi River flowing beneath me on this Bealtaine sunrise is moving forever forward, relentlessly delivering upstate runoff to the Gulf of Mexico, it is also home to the ages, changing and evolving as they may.

Egrets and herons and bald eagles still nest here, and migratory Canada geese and tropical birds follow its flyway like an ancient road, twice each year, just like they always have. Now at Bealtaine, the spring birds are returning, just like they did last year and for the eons before that.

The sun is slipping slowly northward again, the days lengthening. Time is expanding before my eyes.

14. Thoreau, Henry David. *Walden, or Life in the Woods.* New York: Signet Classics, 1999. (Original publication 1854): p. 78

Chapter 5

Summer Solstice:
Animals Shape the Human World

THE SUMMER SOLSTICE

AT FIVE IN THE morning, the dawn is interrupted by the rush and pounding of a train lumbering at the base of the Julien Dubuque Monument bluff, its headlights sweeping across the Catfish Creek bridge in the last few moments of darkness. Its horn blast disrupts the morning sounds.

But after the train passes, the general ruckus of life at high summer returns. Last night's crickets are still grinding away while the cardinals have wakened with their signature call, "Birdie, Birdie, Birdie." A pair of geese pounds out of the mist on the far shore like airborne bowling pins. At the exact moment of sunrise, 5:35 a.m., a fishing boat plows a V down the middle of the stilled river en route to a favorite walleye hole. The Midsummer Day's humidity will bring out mosquitos, which in turn will excite the bats at the closing of the longest day of the year.

At Dubuque's latitude the solstice daylight will last fifteen hours, with a half-hour warmup and wind-down on either side. Sixteen bright hours teeming with squirrels, deer, ticks, robins, chipmunks, dogs, cattle, sheep, geese, rattlesnakes, field mice, flies, splash of leaping bass, egrets heaving their long, tired wings like bellows, and turtles sunning on river logs.

This one we love, this one we admire, this one we fear.

Animals shape the human world. It's us and them together, and no one else on this deep blue planet whirling through the darkness.

COUNTY MAYO

I had been in Westport, County Mayo, only a week before I received a response to my inquiry about the Westport Hillwalking and Mountaineering Club. Visitors and newbies were invited to join in on two "Easy" level hikes before joining the group permanently, and I obliged by making arrangements to meet the hike leader, Brian, at the Westport Quay.

It was Easter Monday and the centennial commemoration of the 1916 Easter Rising, and while Dublin was celebrating with a gigantic parade and a host of historic remembrances, western Ireland took to hillwalking. A busload of hikers from nearby Newport were going to trace the route of local rebellion leaders. Other walks were annual events: Christian and post-Christian pilgrimages following old religious routes, all part of Ireland's National Pilgrim Path Week. The Westport Hillwalking Club had scheduled multiple hikes, but I'm glad I selected Brian's, as we struck up a friendship that included additional hikes, bicycling, and coffee house chats.

We would be hiking the Children of Lir Loop in northern County Mayo. I had not yet ventured far in my rented car, and so was thankful when Brian invited me to ride with him on the hour-long drive. We headed north, then west, of Westport on the N59, following the Great Western Greenway bike trail I had already ridden, and we met up with more hikers who joined our caravan at Newport. At Mulranny, the N59 took a sharp turn north into territory I hadn't yet explored.

I plied Brian and his hiking companion with questions as we drove through the uninhabited bogs past the Ballycroy National Park. Had the countryside always been this unpopulated, or were there small farmers here before the Famine? Is this patch of peat naturally eroded, or cut long ago for turf? He in turn was the first to ask me in both puzzled and jesting tone what would soon become a daily coffee house refrain from the Irish: What's up in America with Donald Trump?

Finally we took another turn, onto the narrow-laned R314, deep into Gaeltacht (Irish-speaking) territory. We parked at a building called An Seanscoil (the Old School), in the village gathering of houses called Ceatru Taidg (Carroweige), and headed as a friendly and conversational group onto the Children of Lir loop as far north on the Mayo coastline as land permits.

The walk takes its name from the mythological home of one of Celtic Ireland's most iconic and lyrical legends, the story of the Children of Lir. The legend suggests the deep Celtic interconnection between humans and the animal world and illustrates the principle of shape-shifting in which humans, by will or by spell, cross over into the animal world and return again.

Lir was a fairy-king, a ruler of the sea, happily married to a mortal, Aoibh [Eve], who bore him a daughter and three sons. Aoibh died in childbirth while delivering the last son. Lir soon remarried, this time to Aoibh's sister, Aoife [E-fa]. Over time, Aoife grew jealous of Lir's warm, fatherly relationship with his children, so she turned the children into swans, cursed for the next nine hundred years until the sound of bells would release them. They were to spend three hundred years on Lough Derravaragh near their home in County Meath, three hundred years on the Straits of Moyle between Northern Ireland and Scotland battling the raging seas, and their final three hundred years on a small lake on the island Inish Glora, off the coast of County Mayo, where we were hiking.

Although the spell had turned the children into swans, it hadn't stolen their voices. The swan-children sang beautiful songs together to keep their spirits up. Their swan voices eventually alerted Lir to their fate. He banished their stepmother, Aoife, and lived among his swan children for their first three hundred years, whereupon the swans moved on to the next location of their curse, and King Lir went on to his death.

Like all legends, alternate versions of the story exist, and some of these were further altered by the Christian monks who first wrote down the Celtic myths. In one version of the story, in the third location, off the coast of Mayo, the swans heard church bells ringing, signaling that Saint Patrick had come to Ireland and the end of their curse was near. The swans followed the pealing bells to the monastic hut of a monk named Caemhog [CAVE-og], who cared for them as their time of transformation neared. Before their time arrived, however, a king of Connacht appeared at the monk's hut, demanding the singing swans for himself. The monk resisted and tolled the bells one more time, whereupon a mist overtook the lake and the swans shape-shifted back into children.

The story has no happy ending, however, except perhaps to the Celtic Christian monks who had shape-shifted the legend to their will in the first place. The children, like Oisin after leaving Tír na nÓg, instantly aged their nine hundred years, surviving only long enough to be baptized by Caemhog before passing away into legend.

We saw no swans on our hike, let alone singing swans. The Irish definition of an "easy" hike doesn't quite match mine, and the four-hour walk took us climbing up some steep-sloped bogs and down some deep ravines. We walked along the Black Ditch, a sod fence built up over the centuries to keep sheep from falling over the cliff face into the Atlantic. We zipped up our jackets and waterproofs against a brief pelting rain that welled up from the sea and let loose on the treeless coastline ridge. And we unbundled again when the sun reappeared just in time for a golden showing of the rugged, weather-beaten ledges that had collapsed, in geologic time, to form Kid Island. Finally, we emerged at the Children of Lir sculpture that marks the turning point where the trail heads inland. No singing swans here, but the sculpture offered instead a set of melodious pipes which we thwacked with our hiking sticks to create our own haunting tune.

We settled in for lunch in a sun-filled mountain valley bisected by an even more-melodious mountain creek. My new colleagues playfully but unsuccessfully prodded me to recite poetry for them as their most recent new hillwalker had done, but my memory had gone blank and I couldn't figure out how to beg off that I'm mostly a prose man.

Hours later we returned to the town of Carroweige and wound down with tea and coffee and good laughs in the dark pub rooms of Teach O'Conghoile's [House of O'Connell]. Brian and his hiking companion got us lost on the drive home, for which I was silently grateful, as I absorbed the north County Mayo shoreline and back roads from the back seat and filed them away in memory for a later return visit on my own.

We saw a few hawks and seabirds riding the wind during our hike. But it took another walk into the writings of Ireland's premier contemporary nature writer and Mayo resident, Michael Viney, for me to *see* what I had seen on the Children of Lir landscape, as well to see what I had missed. Viney, who for fifty years has been an *Irish Times* nature columnist and is author of the comprehensive *Ireland: A Smithsonian Natural History*, has focused his observant eyes on Ireland's west coast in *Wild Mayo*. The county's wildlife habitat, he explains, includes harbour seals along its Atlantic coast; skylarks and lizards and grouse in the peatlands; relict vertigo snails in the watery fens, whose species date from glacial times; white-fronted geese and goldeneye ducks in the lakelands; pochard ducks in the turloughs; snowy owls on the islands; pine martens and long-eared owls in the forests; and minks and crayfish and salmon in the rivers. Although not animals per se, certain bog plants like sundews and butterworts have adopted carnivorous ways, trapping insects on their sticky leaves for a slow devouring of their nutrients.[1]

And, not far from the Children of Lir Loop, Termoncarragh Lake provides a winter refuge for mate-for-life whooper swans[2] that may or may not be embodying shape-shifted human couples.

Viney attributes County Mayo's rich diversity of wildlife to the "extremely varied geology of the county's mountain rim, shaped and scarred by glacial action, plus a growth-promoting, oceanic climate." Likewise, he adds, the intimate scale of the human countryside—with its small fields, stone walls, earthen banks and hedgerows resulting from a heritage of subsistence farming—preserves habitats "that would have been swept away in a more developed landscape."[3]

But County Mayo wildlife, like creatures anywhere, faces severe environmental threats, some common to the globe, some unique to its particular landscape. Vanishing bog and peatland, climate change, agricultural and mono-cultured forest runoff, and increased incidence of algae blooms all pose threats to Mayo's wildlife. And, ironically, solutions to one environmental problem may beget another, according to Viney. Conifer forests first planted on marginal land by the government and now by farmers with state incentives to create carbon sinks will "reduce the habitats of open countryside of high environmental value and threaten further reduction in scarce birds such as the hen harrier."[4] But at the same time, the forest carbon sinks provide some local wildlife benefit as well, writes Viney: "Greater bird variety persists at the fringes of mature forest and it shelters more spiders, wood mice, and lichens."[5]

Nothing, it seems, is extremely simple.

On the positive side, Viney points out various environmental designations that have helped to preserve Mayo species. About one-fourth of County Mayo offers species protection in Natural Heritage Areas, Special Areas of Conservation, and Special Protection Areas.

Poet Sean Lysaght of Westport also writes extensively of birdlife in northern County Mayo. In a recent essay published in the *Dublin Review*, Lysaght discusses the reintroduction of sea eagles to western Ireland. Once

1. Viney, *Wild Mayo*.
2. Viney, *Wild Mayo*, 36-37.
3. Viney, Email Correspondence.
4. Viney, Email Correspondence.
5. Viney, Email Correspondence.

plentiful along the coastline, the sea eagles went into decline by the late 1890s. In 1898, Richard James Ussher visited Mayo while gathering information for his 1900 book, *Birds of Ireland*, and wrote that they were "on the point of extinction." According to Lysaght, "The sea eagles . . . held out until 1909, but when Ussher returned in 1910 he was unable to prove breeding; after that, the records fall silent."[6]

A reintroduction of Norway sea eagles that began in 2007 has been controversial to some locals who view the raptors as sheep-killers. Some reintroduced eagles have been found poisoned, although it is impossible to know whether the poison was intended for the eagles or for other unwanted animals, such as foxes. Despite setbacks, sea eagles have been successfully reintroduced in at least four locations in western Ireland. The first successful breeding of re-introduced sea eagles was at Lough Derg in County Clare in 2013, not far from County Mayo, where six pairs raised seven chicks. The first eagles to grace Killarney National Park in over one hundred years had successfully bred chicks by summer 2015.[7]

I did not know, I could not know, the Mayo landscape and its animal wildlife with as much depth and intimacy as Michael Viney, Sean Lysaght, or Brian and my Children of Lir hillwalking companions. But I was all eyes, all ears, as absorbent as peatland moss. These were new places to me, alien landscapes becoming more familiar with each long hike and conversation, and while some of the wildlife and some of the habitation threats and successes were unique to County Mayo, they were in other ways not so different from back home.

But while Ireland today is faced with the same modern alienation from the natural world as plagues my own home, I can't help but wonder if its deep historical and cultural ties to the landscape and the creatures of the earth will give it an edge over the North American Driftless, where the Euro-American cultural connection to nature runs skin deep in time and where the Native culture with deep-time ties to the landscape was largely displaced.

How, then, might I, who can't tell a sparrow from a wren, come to understand North American animals as earth companions? On a Mississippi backwater could I shapeshift into an egret and trail my legs behind me?

6. Lysaght, "The Eagle and the Precipice," 9.

7. Lucey, "First sea eagle chicks in one hundred years take flight in Kerry."

ANIMALS SHAPE THE HUMAN WORLD

Animal imagery is deeply woven into the mythologies of both pre-Christian and Christian Celtic Ireland, reflecting the rural nature of ancient Irish society. But the role of animals in these tales departs from the strict human/animal dichotomy that frequents Western thought. While sea monsters and ravens still wreaked havoc on the human world, other animals came to the aid of humans and carried messages from the Divine. Animals and humans formed a communion in the Celtic world. In the ultimate act of union, humans and animals frequently shape-shifted into each other's forms, whether for safety or by way of a beautiful curse.

Foremost among the animals who shape the human experience is the salmon, thought by the Celts to be the oldest and wisest of creatures. The Celts' strong affinity to place lore led them to revere the salmon, which always finds its way back home. In Celtic mythology, the boy-servant Fionn Mac Cumhaill [Finn McCool] splatters his thumb with hot salmon oil while frying up a catch of wisdom for his druidic master. When he sucks his thumb to relieve the pain, he ingests the salmon's wisdom, and transforms into a heroic warrior who, when thereafter putting his thumb to his mouth, can see the past, present, and future all at once.

Another symbolic animal in Celtic mythology was the swan, which represented beauty and grace overlying strength and fierceness.[8] In a typical tale, a swan maiden, half-swan and half-human, leaves her plumage on a lakeshore to swim naked in human form. A man finding (and hiding) her plumage may marry the beautiful woman, but she has more rights than a human wife, and should her terms be violated or should she find her plumage, she may become a swan again and fly away.

On the dark side, the raven was linked to the deathly war-goddess Morrigan. The raven encourages bloody engagement, appropriate and advantageous to the carrion-consuming bird. The raven may also recite oracles, such as premonitions of who will die in the next day's battle. But sometimes the raven is simply a bird of ill omen. When young Deirdre, the reluctant intended bride of Ulster's King Concobar, sees a crow sipping blood from the snow, she pines to find and fall in love instead with some other man with hair as black as the raven's, skin as fair as the snow, and lips as red as the blood. When she finds and falls in love with such a man, the young couple flee the king's wrath but are eventually killed.

8. Melia, "Animals and Birds in Celtic Tradition."

Even domesticated animals shape the human world in Celtic mythology. Cattle were not only the primary measure of wealth in Celtic Ireland, but were descended from goddesses, such as Bó Find, a white cow goddess who with her sisters (the red and black cows) arose from the western sea and crossed inland, "creating life behind them as they traveled."[9]

But it is the ability of humans to shape-shift into animals—by special powers or under curse—that cements the companion relationship of humans and animals in Celtic lore. Sabd, a beautiful young woman, is turned into a deer by one of her father's druidic rivals, but when Fionn Mac Cumhaill spares her in a hunt, she slips back into human form at night to become his lover. When the druid finds out, he turns her into a deer forever.

Shape-shifting also occurred for protection or to pursue the hunt. When the hero Cian mac Cainte is outnumbered by three warriors, he turns himself into a boar—symbol of prowess in battle—to intensify his attack against them. The warriors in turn shape-shift into dogs, better able to bring down the boar in battle.[10]

Irish Benedictine monk Seán Ó Duinn argues that shape-shifting in Celtic mythology represents "the *neart*, the creative energy going out from God, ever present, ever changing."[11] In *Where Three Streams Meet*, O'Duinn tells the following shape-shifting legend brimming with the energy of transformable life. The Celtic goddess Ceridwen brews an herb potion to turn her ugly son into a brilliant druid and poet, but, much like in the story of Fionn Mac Cumhaill, her boy-servant Gwion Bach is splattered with the potion, puts his hand to his mouth to ease the pain, and ingests the wisdom intended for Ceridwen's son. Ó Duinn tells the shape-shifting aftermath with as much verve as any Celtic bard:

> Ceridwen jumped at him to kill him but Gwion Bach turned himself into a hare and ran away from her. She turned herself into a greyhound and pursued him. He reached the sea and jumped in to avoid her and he became a fish. She jumped in after him and became an otter. Just as he was about to be caught he turned himself into a bird and soared up into the air. She turned herself into a hawk and soared above him. Then he saw beneath him on the ground a heap of corn, which a farmer had been threshing. He swooped down and became a grain of corn. But Ceridwen

9. Monaghan, *Encyclopedia of Celtic Mythology and Folklore*, 52.

10. The preceding animal mythologies are derived from Monaghan, *Encyclopedia of Celtic Mythology and Folklore*.

11. Ó Duinn, *Where Three Streams Meet*, 86

swooped down too and became a hen. She gobbled up all the corn and thought that this was the end of Gwion Bach. Then she turned herself into a woman again and found she was pregnant. Nine months later, she had a son and from his infancy he was full of all the wisdom and learning of the ages — this, of course, was Gwion Bach who came back again in human form after all his various transformations and he became known as Taliesin, the great poet of Wales whose fame lives on to this day among Celts.[12]

Celtic Christian mythology retained this intimacy with the animal world, with a subtle shift toward viewing animals as helpmates, as messengers from God, or simply as worthy of respect and protection in their own regard.

In *The Life of Patrick*, an eighth-century hagiography of the saint, Patrick and his followers shape-shift, or at least appear to, when nearing an ambush set up by his pagan enemies: "The king was counting them as they approached, when in an instant he could no longer see them. All that the pagans could see was eight deer and a fawn going as if to the desert."[13]

St. Brigit enlists the abundance of animals in service to the poor. Sent out to milk the cows and make butter for her mother, the young Brigit instead gives the milk and butter away to the poor and to travelers. Aware that she has nothing to bring home, she prays, whereupon the cow produces abundantly more milk again for Brigit's home.[14] The story echoes the imagery of the pre-Christian tale of Glas, the mythological cow of great abundance who could wander about the entire island of Ireland in a single day and feed everyone according to their needs.[15]

Brigit mythology shows her compassion toward animals and fellow humans alike. When a man kills the king's pet fox, having mistaken it for a wild animal, Brigit saves him from the king's rage by offering the king a new fox which had willingly offered itself to Brigit for the occasion. Later, the sly fox—perhaps with Brigit's blessing—manages its own escape and returns to the wild. According to the seventh-century *Life of St. Brigit*, "All animals, flocks, and birds were subject to her will."[16]

---

12. Ó Duinn, *Where Three Streams Meet*, 86.

13. Davies, *Celtic Spirituality*, 102.

14. Davies, *Celtic Spirituality*, 123-124

15. Monaghan, *Encyclopedia of Celtic Mythology and Folklore*, 215.

16. Davies, *Celtic Spirituality*, 129-130.

After Patrick and Brigit, Ireland's third patron saint—Columbkille—likewise carries on the Celtic interaction with the animal world. Evoking Christ-imagery among the world of animals at his Iona monastery off the coast of Scotland, the Irish-born St. Columbkille calls a fellow monk to him and foretells that a weary crane, blown off course by heavy winds, will land on Iona's coast three days hence. The monk is instructed to care for the crane, nurse it, and feed it for three days until it regains its strength and flies away to Ireland.[17] Columbkille even commands the Loch Ness monster, ordering it to desist its attack on a man: "You will go no further; do not touch the man; go back with all speed."[18]

While animals shape the human world in Celtic lore, the Celtic Christian tradition adds the human protection of animals. When a blackbird lands and nests on Glendalough's St. Kevin's outstretched hand during prayer, he stills himself for the next six weeks, his arm like a tree branch, until the egg hatches and the young bird flies away.

But St. Brendan the Navigator perhaps outdoes all other Celtic Christian saints in mythological encounters with animals. In *The Voyage of Brendan*, he and his seafaring monks start a cooking fire on an island that begins to "heave like a wave." The monks are fearful, but Brendan discovers that the island is simply a friendly, helpful whale, "nothing other than a sea animal, the foremost of all that swim in the oceans."[19] Brendan and the monks return annually thereafter, at the Easter Vigil, to say Mass upon the whale's back.

Brendan summons animals to his and his monks' defense: "One day they saw a creature of immense size following them at a distance; it blew spray from its nostrils and cut through the waves at high speed as if coming to devour them," but Brendan calms his monks, prays to God, and after his "pleas for deliverance, another sea monster, appearing from the west, rushed to meet the first animal and, spewing fire from its jaws, immediately attacked it."[20] In another such story, the monks are under attack by a gryphon when a pair of mythic birds come to their defense, one rescuing the monks by seizing them with its talons and the other "[tearing] out the eyes of the gryphon."[21]

17. Sellner, *Wisdom of the Celtic Saints*, 94.

18. Sellner, *Wisdom of the Celtic Saints*, 93.

19. Davies, *Celtic Spirituality*, 163.

20. Davies, *Celtic Spirituality*, 174-175

21. Davies, *Celtic Spirituality*, 179.

In short, the mythologies of the Celtic Christian saints in reference to the animal world are no less numerous nor fantastical than those of their pre-Christian forefathers, suggesting how intimately Celtic Christian life was tied to the natural world and how deeply they regarded the natural world as mystery. Although the stuff of legend, "this attitude of deep respect for the environment was also manifest in their quiet care for all living things . . . Animals are portrayed as fellow creatures of the earth, and once befriended, they become helpers to the saints," writes Edward Sellner.[22]

Perhaps no other Christian tradition and mythology, save that of St. Francis of Assisi, consistently interacts with the animal world with such respect, tenderness, and collaboration as that of the early Celtic Christians. Other Christian traditions at their best have focused on social justice and the needs of individual souls, and at their worst on consolidation of power, theological warring, and repressive and/or abusive attitudes toward human sexuality, but rarely, until the last few decades, on celebration and preservation of the creation itself.

Sounding every bit like a Celtic Christian monk, Pope Francis extolls humanity's moral obligation to the preservation of species in his 2015 encyclical, *Laudato Sí*. Animals, he says, have value unto themselves, praise God in their own ways, and contribute to human good:

> It is not enough, however, to think of different species merely as potential "resources" to be exploited, while overlooking the fact that they have value in themselves. Each year sees the disappearance of thousands of plant and animal species which we will never know, which our children will never see, because they have been lost for ever. The great majority become extinct for reasons related to human activity. Because of us, thousands of species will no longer give glory to God by their very existence, nor convey their message to us. We have no such right.[23]

§ § §

"Who is wiser than one who knows the way home?" asks Patricia Monaghan, linking Ireland's salmon to those of her Alaskan home where intimacy with nature is just a step out the door.[24] But as I examine my own Midwestern Driftless tradition, I find little intimacy or mythology connected to the

22. Sellner, *Wisdom of the Celtic Saints*, 22.

23. Pope Francis, *Laudato Sí*, Parag. 33.

24. Monaghan, *The Red-Haired Girl from the Bog*, 190.

animal world, except for a few European-inherited associations such as the slyness of foxes, the wisdom of owls, and the grace and beauty of deer. To some degree this disconnection results from a predatory relationship with the landscape. But to an equal degree, it simply reflects Euro-American settlement in a scientific age. For the most part, in my neck of the river valley, a walleye is a walleye and a carp is a carp. Aside for their traits as edible or hardly edible, no lore accompanies the existence of animals in a Midwestern pragmatics-driven culture.

Native American culture was and is steeped in animal lore, of course. Effigy Mounds National Monument in northeast Iowa, with its burial and ceremonial mounds in the shapes of bears and birds, hints at ancient Native American loric animal associations. Bears are typically symbols of strength and moral behavior, inhabiting the underworld in winter and the surface world in summer. Eagles, inhabiting the upperworld, have healing and hunting powers, serving as messengers between the Creator and humans. In the 1,000-year-old Marching Bears configuration that graces the Mississippi River bluff at Effigy Mounds, ten bear mounds, marching southward, are flanked by three birds, presumably eagles. One of the eagles flies near the end of the line of bears, while two eagles are out front, leading the way.

In contrast, the two-century-old Euro-American culture of the Driftless offers little symbolic relationship to the animal world. But the best among us—not all, of course, but many—respect the animals they work with and recognize our interdependence. My good friend Eric Anglada, a former land caretaker along with his wife Brenna at New Hope Catholic Worker Farm before setting out at Saint Isidore Catholic Worker Farm, says, "At New Hope Farm, animals were in some sense community. I was in charge of the chickens. They took care of us by giving us eggs, and I took care of them by feeding them and protecting them from predators. They shaped my day, made me mindful of the daylight. Our rhythms were shaped by the lives of the animals, tending to and being responsible for them." Even slaughtering animals for food was sacred: "We would thank them for their lives."[25]

If animals shape the human world in Celtic lore, there is no denying that humans shape—or misshape—animal habitat in the modern world. But the Midwest's—if not America's—most prominent voice for a right relationship between humans and the natural world, including the world of animals, was Aldo Leopold, whose famous "shack" sat on the edge of the

25. Anglada, Personal Interview.

Driftless in the so-called sand counties of southwest Wisconsin. In his essay "Thinking Like a Mountain," published as part of *A Sand County Almanac* in 1949, he realized with unfortunate hindsight that his early forestry days of eradicating wolves from the American Southwest mountains had resulted in forests being stripped of vegetation by predator-free deer. He writes, "I was young then, and full of trigger-itch; I thought that because fewer wolves meant more deer, that no wolves would mean hunters' paradise. But after seeing the green fire [in the eyes of the wolf he shot] die, I sensed that neither the wolf nor the mountain agreed."[26]

Later he would shape his views into a "land ethic" which presented the natural world—the land and its creatures—as an equal member of the world community in which humans operate:

> The land ethic simply enlarges the boundaries of the community to include soils, waters, plants, and animals, or collectively: the land. [It] changes the role of *Homo sapiens* from conqueror of the land-community to plain member and citizen of it. It implies respect for his fellow-members, and also respect for the community.[27]

Put simply—and fluidly—"A thing is right when it tends to preserve the integrity, stability, and beauty of the biotic community. It is wrong when it tends otherwise."[28]

There are no salmon in the Mississippi River, no deeply ingrained mythologies explaining our cultural relationship to the animals inhabiting the landscape. But there are voices calling for us to live in right relationship to the natural world—whether we call the animals brethren or not—for our own human good, if for no other sake.

YELLOW RIVER STATE FOREST

Even an overcast mid-October morning beams with golden light in a Driftless woods, where half of the yellowing leaves still cling to the branches while the other half litter the forest floor. In a breeze they will light up the space between.

---

26. Leopold, *A Sand County Almanac*, 130.

27. Leopold, *A Sand County Almanac*, 204.

28. Leopold, *A Sand County Almanac*, 224.

Bird biologist Jon Stravers[29] and I are bounding through the leaf-strewn dirt roads of the Yellow River State Forest north of Marquette, Iowa, bouncing over a few ruts and pausing occasionally to peer through the woods to spot the old oaks and hickories where Jon tracks cerulean warblers each spring and summer. But in general our movement is upward, ascending through the forest en route to the Cedar Point overlook above Paint Creek where Jon has constructed, rock by rock, a 500-stone raptor effigy.[30]

Parking where the road ends fifty yards from the overlook, we swish through fallen leaves till we emerge at the cliff-face with its view clear to the east, save for one tenacious old cedar clinging to the limestone edge. ("That gnarly old dog, how long do you think he's been here?" Jon rasps.) Before us lies the 35-foot wing-spanned stone raptor, its left wing a dozen feet from the overlook. It looks much lighter than its rocky weight.

Located in northeast Iowa along the Mississippi River just an eagle's glide from Effigy Mounds National Monument, the Yellow River State Forest where Jon has assembled his stone sculpture protects 8,600 acres of pine and oak/hickory hardwoods, along with maples, elms, cottonwoods, basswoods and conifers, as well as patches of restored prairie.

But Yellow River is also a "working forest" with an annual yield of more than $80,000 in timber sales and a sophisticated timber management plan Department of Natural Resources (DNR) conservation practices are designed to keep the forest healthy and lumber-productive indefinitely.

Many of northeast Iowa's oak and hickory hardwood forests took root 150 years ago after hillsides had been denuded for railroads, construction, and heating fuel. After lumber interests turned their attention elsewhere, new hardwood seedlings thrived under the sun, and the forest slowly revived. These hardwoods have now reached their life expectancy, but their seedlings struggle in the dense mix of competing forest species. Ironically, Iowa's forest soils are so fertile that good lumber species find themselves at a disadvantage, says Robert Honeywell, then Area Forester at Yellow River State Forest. Everything under the sun and shade likes to grow in an Iowa forest, but that creates a lot of competition in the woods. "Oak and hickory

29. All conversations with Jon Stravers derive from a 21 October 2015 personal interview and/or from my earlier essay featuring Jon, "Mississippi Refuge," from *The Driftless Land*.

30. Jon has since moved his stone raptor to another northeast Iowa Mississippi River bluff outside the state forest.

don't regenerate under their parent species," he points out. "They need open canopy."[31]

Yellow River State Forest officials use an Even-Aged Management system to keep the forest vital. Private loggers will clear-cut a section, ordinarily about three acres, and management officials will replant oak, hickory and pine. With an annual harvest of about forty acres, much of the forest can be culled and replanted on roughly a 100-year rotation. "The goal," says Honeywell, "is to improve the composition and overall health of the forest."

Yellow River Forest is home to a wide range of mammals, including white tailed deer, wild turkeys, squirrels, rabbits, grouse, mink, river otters, beavers, badgers, muskrats, raccoons, opossums, weasels, ground hogs, and coyotes. North-facing algific talus slopes with limestone outcrops that sit atop exposed shale produce cold air vents in summer, offering rare habitat protection for glacial-era relict species like the endangered Pleistocene Snail. And the spacious forest is both home and migratory haven to a wide range of birds, including Cooper's hawks, scarlet tanagers, and Jon Stravers' favorites, the red shouldered hawk and cerulean warbler.[32]

Much of the region encompassing Yellow River State Forest, Effigy Mounds, the Upper Mississippi National Fish & Wildlife Refuge, and Pikes Peak was designated a 35,000-acre Important Bird Area (IBA) in 2014, due in large part to the bird-nesting inventories Stravers conducts for the Audubon Society, the DNR, and other environmental groups and agencies. Stravers' inventories, for example, identified 190 territories of the cerulean warbler, which is in 75% decline nationwide but thriving in the Driftless. The Effigy Mounds-Yellow River IBA provides habitat for over one hundred bird species, including tropical migrants that seasonally inhabit the area. The site also includes nesting sites of rare and reintroduced raptors like the peregrine falcon and the bald eagle.[33]

Across the river, Wyalusing State Park is included in a separate Wisconsin IBA program, adding to the overall bird sanctuary. But, says Jon, "The birds don't pay any attention to political boundaries, and I try to ignore some of that as well."

§ § §

31. Koch, Kevin. "A Real 'Working' Forest." [Yellow River State Forest]. *The Dubuque Telegraph Herald*. 2 December 2012.

32. Yellow River State Forest Management Plan.

33. "Site in NE Iowa will become state's first globally important bird area."

I first met Jon several years ago when he agreed to take me out in his boat on the Mississippi backwaters where he conducts his bird nesting inventories. The river was at flood stage, so we floated among the tree trunks and bounced over a couple of floating logs. Our purpose for the day was to "listen to see who's showing up, who's talking."

Zig-zagging among the trunks, Jon mentioned how he'd once—just once—got the boat wedged between two trees. "Be prepared to be flexible," he told me as we passed among low-lying branches and vines.

Stravers has been conducting bird research here for forty years, his work pieced together with Audubon stipends, grants, and "just plain stubbornness." The bird surveys "pay me to go where I would go anyway." His nesting inventories on red shouldered hawks and now cerulean warblers "keep taking me back into those places where I feel that sense of place."

Stravers explains that the Mississippi became his refuge when he returned from Vietnam in the 1970s. "My return strategy was to get in a canoe and escape," he said. The avocation soon became his vocation. Stravers was introduced to the world of raptors by Gladys Black, "Iowa's bird lady," and soon earned his license for bird banding. Soon Jon was doing bird species surveys for the Audubon Society, the Fish and Wildlife Service, the Army Corps of Engineers, area colleges, and others.

"The red shouldered hawk pulled me in" to the Driftless river shores, says Jon. "I try to decipher their language." In the woods, Jon listens for the style and inflection of the nesting male and female hawks. The male will trill first, with the female responding. From the calls, Jon can locate the nest. He has been known to climb tall oaks and hickories, then, to count the number of eggs in a particular nest.

That first boat outing with Jon achieved its goal when we faintly heard two red shouldered hawks. The second hawk added an extra syllable in response to the first: "kee-yaw, kee-yaw, kee-yaw." The extra syllable meant it's a female, we were near the nest, and she didn't like it. Although we hadn't actually spotted the hawks or seen the nest, Jon said contentedly, "My work is done for the day. I know they're here." Then Jon revved up the boat motor, slid us out of the flooded woods and into the backwaters, and headed for home.

Over time, Stravers began expanding his interest to other species. His son Jon-Jon, following in his father's footsteps as a naturalist until killed in a 2007 car accident "renewed the spiritual bond in me by telling me that I'd been too focused on the red shouldered hawks and wasn't listening to the entire forest. He taught me to slow down, to listen to what I'd been missing." The result since then has been the expansion of Stravers' work to cerulean warblers, a sky-blue, black and white bird about four inches long and weighing less than ½ ounce.

I had kept in touch with Jon only occasionally since our boating expedition, till news of his stone raptor recaptured my attention. After a couple of emails we loaded into Jon's car instead of his boat, and began bouncing our way through the Yellow River Forest.

Stopping occasionally en route to the stone raptor, Jon points to the thirty-inch diameter cottonwoods, ancient oaks and black walnuts that his cerulean warblers inhabit. Their choice of tree "perhaps has something to do with tree structure and topography–open spacing in the upper branches," Jon says, exercising his Audubon thinking. Then Jon engages his mystical side: "Or perhaps it could be the cerulean recognizing the wisdom of an ancient tree."

Cerulean warblers migrate to the Driftless from Venezuela, Colombia, Bolivia, Peru, and the northern Amazon. Jon marvels at the mystery: "How do they find their way over 3,000 miles, a forest bird crossing the Gulf of Mexico trusting the compass in their heart and the elders of their clan?"

The cerulean warblers usually arrive around May 5. "They talk differently when they court, when the eggs are laid, and when their chicks are hatched," Jon explains. After the young reach adolescence, the parents stop singing and the family unit blends into the surrounding clan of warblers. They leave Yellow River by the end of August to return south.

In May and June, as early as 4:30 a.m. Jon is at the Yellow River Forest, at the Sny Magill Effigy Mound unit where Native Americans built mounds at shoreline level instead of on the bluff, or at other lowlands edging the Mississippi so he can be in the best location when first light arrives. He has been tracking about two hundred ceruleans in the region, learning where they nest and how they defend their territories. A female leaving the nest, for example, will hide its location by dropping twenty feet straight down ("bungee jumping," according to Stravers), before taking wing.[34]

Jon is as much caught up in the mystery as the science of migrating birds. "I'm trying to figure out what draws them in, what brings them back." The mystery, for Jon at least, largely resides in the Driftless landscape,

---

34. "Site in NE Iowa will become state's first globally important bird area."

particular the region encompassing the Yellow River State Forest and nearby Effigy Mounds National Monument.

"Something happened to me where I first visited the bird effigies at Effigy Mounds," he says, describing his 1975 first encounter with the 200-foot mounds overlooking the Mississippi. "I loved that view, that feeling, that remoteness when nobody else is up there. There began a longing within me to be close to that place. Though I knew little about the people who built them, I felt connected to them."

His sense of place includes the riverine and inland forests. "Some of these places where I have found the red shouldered hawks and cerulean warblers have the strongest vibes. Maybe it's the birds, the rocks, the vistas, the whole valley."

Jon's passion for the Driftless springs forth through music as well. His band, Big Blue Sky, has recorded six CDs of music written mostly by himself and his son, Jon Jon, with song titles reflective of his sense of place: Universal Mother, Driftless Moon, Bird Dance, and Going Driftless.

But by 2015, Jon's artistic expression of the Driftless took a new direction when he began building the stone raptor on a cliff overlook in the Yellow River State Forest. On his regular travels along the forest roads, he picks up fist- to lap-sized rocks and hauls them to the overlook, where he places them, stone by stone, in the outline or interior of the growing bird. Like the mound-builders who placed heart-stones collected from far away at the center of their effigies, Jon has also collected rocks from Idaho, where his daughter and grandchildren live, and added them to the raptor.

Today Jon pulls a new stone from the back of the car to place on the wing. Some stones, he says, are placed for symbolic value (such as the red stone at the raptor's heart), while the rest are placed for the shape and fitting of the rock. Some bark pieces and small, straight branches give detail to the raptor's tail.

"I come here to become centered," Jon reflects after placing the stone and obliging me with a few photos. "We all need 'spiritual exercise' like we need physical exercise. It only works if you consistently practice it."

Jon sums up his spiritual connection to the Driftless: "You have to have some place that you really know, that you connect to and return to. A lot of people don't have that kind of exercise. Many go to church, and that's great, but being connected to the land is a whole different thing."

So we place our daily stone on the effigy, turn back to the car, and descend through the gray and golden light while the spirit of the raptor takes flight from a Thin Place.

THE PORTAL

There are no salmon in the Upper Mississippi River. My ancestry here in the Driftless has no centuries-deep pools of wisdom for me to draw from. I can't identify species like Jon Stravers or Michael Viney, or like any common birder for that matter.

But when a pair of geese comes bowling out of a Mississippi shoreline mist, honking amid the general bird chatter of the summer solstice dawn when the living world is at its zenith, I know full-deep that we're all in it together, the animals and us, whirling on this blue planet into a dark universe. Whatever is out there, we face as companions, as members of the same earth community whose activities, intentional or not, shape each other's worlds.

Chapter 6

Lughnasa: The Holy Inhabits the Remote, Austere Places

LUGHNASA, AUGUST 1

I RIDE OUT THIS morning by bicycle to the Julien Dubuque Monument, with headlamp and rear flashers accenting the pre-dawn blush of light. It is bright enough to ride safely—but just barely. Luckily, it's only a 15-minute ride from my house to the river bluff. I arrive in plenty of time to sit with Julien and sip some coffee before the 5:55 sunrise. A slight haze lies across the horizon and a fine mist over the river. I wonder whether the sunrise will be obscured behind the haze, but the orange ball burns through and turns, by degrees, yellow and then white.

For it is the first of the dog days of August. In the Driftless these are the days of the white-hot sun and humidity that drenches with the slightest exertion. This is also the driest time of year, when lawns brown out until the autumn rains return.

Alone on this bluff in the desert of late summer, I understand, if only slightly, the compulsion to seek the Holy in the remote and austere places. The solitude I spend watching the rising sun enter and cross the triangular geometry of my bike frame leaned up against a railing reminds me that, sometimes, to be alone is not to be lonely.

I like solitude, but I take mine in small doses. The sun is climbing earnestly now, burning off the haze, and so I get back on the bike and head for home, to Dianne, and the day that awaits.

§ § §

Lughnasa is the Celtic festival of light and of early harvest, celebrated on August 1, the halfway point between the summer solstice and the fall equinox. It is a sun feast. The ancient Celts recognized two gods of the sun, Lugh and Balor. Lugh was a beneficent god, bringing light, life, and warmth to the earth. It was Lugh who mated with the earth goddess Baoi, circling her in a dance each day and lying with her each night, entering the earth through the goddess' holy wells. The earth's bounty was the product of their mating. In competition with Lugh was another sun god, Balor, who wreaked havoc from the skies. Balor was to blame when the sun was too intense and inflicted drought, or hid himself too long so that the crops were stunted in the fields. Balor demanded sacrifice to be kept at bay.[1]

But when the first fruits of the harvest rolled in—the season's new potatoes and a wealth of berries—the Celts knew that Lugh had been victorious over Balor, and the great Festival of Lughnasa began.

Lughnasa has always been a bawdy affair, alit with fairs, mountain treks, and, of course, more bonfires. Youth took to the hills supposedly to pick berries, but more so to revel in the wildness of their rare freedom. Marriages conceived at Lughnasa were trial affairs that could be terminated by husband or wife within the year. Related to Lughnasa were Puck Fairs, held within a few weeks of the ancient feast. The County Kerry town of Kilorglen still holds an annual August Puck Fair in which a captured wild goat is proclaimed King Puck, paraded through town, crowned by a young schoolgirl, and placed on a pedestal of honor for the three lively days of the Gathering, the Fair, and the Dispersal before being released again to the wild. Today's Puck Fair is family-friendly or raucous, depending on the direction one looks. [2]

§ § §

How does a bawdy, early harvest festive transform into a search for the Holy in the remote, austere places? One answer awaits atop the barren, scree-pathed mountain that rises 2,500 feet above Clew Bay in western County Mayo.

On a five-minute walk from my Westport apartment, on the Greenway Great Western walking and bicycling trail, the sharp-angled peak of

---

1. Molloy, *The Globalization of God*, 12-13, 23.

2. Monaghan, *The Red-Haired Girl from the Bog*, 228-231.

Croagh Patrick comes into view and dominates the horizon. The hard, quartzite top of the mountain forms a rough white triangle at the apex.

I climbed Croagh Patrick, also known as the Reek[3], with two visiting American friends, Tom and Barb. We set off on an April Saturday morning at 9 a.m., an Irish weekend hour that virtually assured we'd have the mountain to ourselves. Our talk was light and relaxed as we started the ascent. We gradually peeled off jacket layers, warmed by exertion, and then put them on again when wind gusts and chill returned at higher altitude.

At the end of the mountain's long and gradual shoulder, the climb turned more serious when the faint white trail launched quite vertically up toward the Reek's cone-shaped peak. The path was scree-strewn—irregular slabs of quartzite broken apart by freeze-thaw cycles and endless pedestrians. The loose scree proved treacherous for climbing (and, later, descending), unpredictably sliding out from beneath our footing. Sometimes we'd paw away the loose rubble to find the solid mountain beneath our boots. The steep incline required switchbacking and grasping bedrock protrusions above us to pull ourselves upward.

We separated into three individual paces. Tom, with the most mountain-climbing experience and, for sure, the longest legs, was out front. I was in the middle. Barb followed next. We each stopped from time to time to check on the progress and safety of each other but no doubt to catch our own breaths as well.

Maybe it was the thin mountain air or the rare piercing sunlight playing with my brain cells, but I conceived a little mantra to occupy my climb and center myself, three principles for climbing Croagh Patrick: Walk in the footsteps of those who've gone before you; lean on your hiking stick for support; and seek the solid mountain. I wondered how many tee-shirts I could sell with such a slogan.

Finally after a two-hour climb and one last upward heave, we each in turn spied the roofline of the simple white chapel built a century ago at the mountain top. After gaining the mountain peak, we admired the view over Clew Bay with its 365 islands ("one for each day of the year"). Whale-backed in shape and looking like they might simply swim away, they are bay-flooded drumlins left behind by the glaciers.

We peeked through the windows of the locked chapel. We ate lunch in the chapel's shadow, watching the barren mountains stretch away to the

---

3. Reek is an Irish word for "mountain."

west. We marveled in our luck, as many who climb Croagh Patrick are met at the top by a gauzy fog.

The austerity of Croagh Patrick has attracted seekers through the ages. Near the base of the mountain, Neolithic standing stones align to a winter solstice sunrise that crests the peak, and from the Neolithic-engraved Boheh Stone several miles away, the sun appears to roll perfectly down the Reek's western slope on April 18 and August 24 on its way to sunset. At the top of the mountain, archaeologists recently unearthed a Celtic hillfort of more than thirty huts, and glass beads found at the site date back to the third century BC. The high reaches of the mountain made the Reek a likely site for Lughnasa feasts. Archaeologists have also unearthed a ninth-century Christian oratory church.

In between the Celtic and Christian occupations, of course, came St. Patrick, from whom the Reek takes its present name, Croagh Patrick, the Rock of Patrick. Evoking Christ's desert journey as he embarked on his public ministry, the eighth century *Book of Armagh* tells of Patrick's forty-day fast and seclusion at the top of the Reek, from which he finally descended to begin his Christianizing mission through Ireland. From Croagh Patrick came the apocryphal banishing of snakes from Ireland, the symbolic driving out of evil.

Not everything about the Reek exuded austerity, of course. At Croagh Patrick the sun god and earth goddess are said to have lain in bed together at Lughnasa, and people would climb the mountain during the night to join with them. Although the Roman church denounced the overtly sexual nature of this ritual, the practice was common until recent years.[4]

For others, however, the pre-Christian feast of Lughnasa transformed into the somber Christian observance of Reek Sunday, the last Sunday of July, on which day a throng of up to 15,000 people climb Croagh Patrick. The pilgrimage is undertaken by Christian penitents, some of whom climb the mountain barefoot, and by the secular who turn out for the grand communal event.

Beyond Reek Sunday, 100,000 people climb Croagh Patrick each year. Almost every weekend brings a crowd by mid-day. The mountain trail has eroded badly. The naturally-occurring scree loosens even more under the feet of endless climbers, and the mountain paths widen as climbers try to avoid the deeply-trodden, rain-washed ruts.

---

4. Malloy, Email Correspondence.

No doubt it is ironic and self-defeating to seek the remote alongside 100,000 other climbers. But the remote and the austere is not always a physical place, and the intense concentration required to maintain solid footing amid Croagh Patrick's loose scree takes me, at least, to the remote places within. Small talk among companions withers to interior thoughts and then dissolves to no thoughts whatsoever, a blankness of mind as faint and piercing as a mountaintop sun.

There I find my Lughnasa. Remote and austere, the interior self is also a locus of the sun, the harvest, and always something still bounding wild.

THE ARAN ISLANDS

Dara Molloy and his wife Tess meet me off the ferry on Inishmore, the largest of the Aran Islands off of Ireland's west coast. I had ferried in from Doolin where I had been exploring the Burren for the past few days. Dara himself had just returned home by ferry from Rossaveal, near Galway. He'd been in Dublin over the weekend performing a Celtic funeral ceremony.

Dara tosses his baggage into the bed of the pickup and tells me to climb in alongside Tess, who is driving. From the back seat Dara engages me in small-talk. Beneath his questions I wonder whether he is trying to figure out why I'd sat on a boat for an hour and a half to talk with a self-described Celtic priest and monk.

Back at his and Tess' house, Dara brews some coffee and shares a loaf of brown bread that Tess has made for his return. Then he settles in at the kitchen table and explains that his own journey to becoming a Celtic monk after arriving in the Aran Islands over thirty years ago echoed the wandering, desert experiences of the ancient Celtic Christian monks. In the Celtic monastic tradition, young monks often wandered before they settled down, "looking for their place of resurrection," Dara says. They weren't looking to colonize or proselytize, but to find that place that would speak to them. Young monks might live for a while as hermits "to perfect their lives and work on themselves" before joining or starting a monastic community. "The best thing you can do for another person," Dara adds, "is to get your own life right."[5]

§ § §

5. Molloy, Personal Interview.

The Arans are a group of three small islands—Inishmore, Inishmaan, and Inisheer—located just beyond Galway Bay. They are extensions of the Burren's glacially-scraped, limestone pavement landscape, but were cut off from the mainland by the rising waters of glacial melt twelve thousand years ago.

Rocky and nearly treeless outposts, for thousands of years they have harbored a hardy people who fished the stormy Atlantic in tarred canvas rowboats called currachs and who gradually built up a thin soil on the islands for pasture and potato fields by mixing seaweed, sand, fishmeal, and manure, and spreading the concoction over small sections of bedrock.

The land and climate are harsh. The islands are buffeted by storms through much of the year. But the landscape is mystical as well. The Atlantic relentlessly and hypnotically pounds the islands' west-facing 300-foot sheer cliffs that drop away into the swells. The porous limestone near sea level creates puffing holes through which the Atlantic upwells and subsides, breathing in and out. Off the gently-sloping, more sedate east shores facing Galway Bay, seals play in the rare sunshine.

Human habitation of the harsh, weathered islands dates at least to Neolithic times, with 4,500-year-old megalithic tombs the oldest surviving structures.

Several years ago my wife and I visited the Inishmore in the April off-season when we had the island more or less to our own touristic selves. We rented bicycles and pedaled to the usual sites, including Dun Aengus (Dun Aonghasa), a late Bronze-Age stone fort constructed around 1500 BC that clings precariously to the island's west cliff face. Its C-shaped stone walls—tiered along the inside curve—protect an enclosure whose straight-line edge plunges three hundred feet into the Atlantic. The grounds are further protected outside the walls by sharp, upended stones called chevaux-de-frise that would slow any advancing attackers. But whether the structure served primarily as a fort or as ceremonial grounds is unknown. Celtic druids later expanded the structure. On a clear night, their bonfires from the rocky ledge would have been visible southward to the County Clare coast.

Dozens of other pre-Christian sites dot the islands as well. After wandering about Dun Aengus and peering over the drop-off ledge, my wife and I set out to find Dúcathair, the Black Fort, abandoning our rented bikes and climbing carefully among the stone-walled fences. The Black Fort proved elusive amid the maze of fences, but we discovered instead purple wildflowers outwitting the limestone pavement and a prancing, penned horse curious to find two wandering humans so far from the road. Meanwhile, the

Black Fort kept retreating into the glare of the afternoon sun. The island, we decided, would show us what it willed, not what we sought.

The harshness of the wet, stony islands attracted early Celtic-Christian ascetics determined to eke out a life of toil and prayer to kindle their own interior fires before gathering a group of monks around themselves. St. Enda founded a monastery named Cille Einne on Inishmore in 490 AD. The monks who trained there went on to establish other monasteries throughout Ireland and beyond. Sixth-century St. Cavan, himself possibly a student of Enda, secluded himself on Inisheer, the smallest island, before building a monastery there. Over time, its stone structures were buried in the billowing sand, but today are excavated. A young St. Columbkille is likewise said to have visited briefly at Enda's monastery and afterward asked for a bit of land to begin his own community. In a fit of monastic jealousy, as the legend goes, Enda refused to give him any land larger than the size of Columbkille's cloak. When Columbkille then tossed the cloak to the ground in anger, the cloak grew and spread to cover the entire island. Enda, infuriated, banished Columbkille from Inishmore, whereupon the latter established numerous monasteries elsewhere throughout Ireland and Scotland, the most famous at Iona, another austere, remote island off the coast of Scotland and the eventual birthplace of the Book of Kells. Columbkille is also said to have cursed Inishmore: as a result, Inishmore would forever be devoid of trees.

Rebuffed by wandering paths, stone fences, and prickly bushes as we tried to approach the Black Fort that seemed always out of sight and out of reach, we eventually returned to our bikes and headed back down the road in the opposite direction. On the southeastern coast, the ocean front flattens into a sandy plain, and near the end of the island chance brought us to the graveyard of Cille Einne, said to hold the remains of Enda and his monks. Our eyes were stopped by a field of grasses with tips brushing in the wind among the Cille Einne Celtic crosses. On the stony island the grasses looked as lush as a Midwestern prairie.

§ § §

Dara Molloy came to the Aran Islands in 1985. At the time an ordained Catholic priest, he had grown increasingly frustrated by the Church's hierarchy and institutional structures. He took a leave of absence from the priesthood and moved to Inishmore, which he had first visited a few years prior. In his book *The Globalization of God*, Molloy writes, "The values I was drawn to were simplicity in lifestyle, hospitality, solidarity with people who were in poverty or suffering injustice, closeness to nature and an all-encompassing resistance to some of the major motivating forces in the world today . . . To my surprise I had begun to see that religious life did not allow me to do that."[6]

The day after Molloy had settled in on Inishmore, he was welcomed by the postman, also named Dara. When Molloy pointed out the connection—ironic in a sense, for two Dara's, named for the oak, to live on an island largely devoid of trees—the postman pointed to a distant island called Oileán Mhic Dara, where the sixth-century St. MacDara had lived as a hermetic monk. "That is where your name and my name comes from," said the postman.[7]

As Molloy contemplated the oak and the remote islands as the source of his name and spiritual center, his private journey took new directions. He reflected on the early Celtic Christians: St. Brigit who had established her monastery at Kildare, the Church of the oaks, and Columbkille, who established his monastery at Doire, "a place of oaks." He was whisked back further to pre-Christian times. "For the Druids, the oak was a mystical doorway to the divine," writes Molloy, and "to be a channel for the divine . . . is something that my whole life has been about."[8]

Molloy felt that he could not live the kind of spiritual life he wanted as a Catholic priest, or as a Catholic, and so he left the Church and priesthood in 1996. Finding his own "place of resurrection," he embraced the Celtic past, married, and began life as a Celtic priest and monk.

Gradually Dara moved beyond a monotheistic view of the world. Offering more bread and coffee at his kitchen table, he explains, "Polytheism is a way of naming the diversity in one's lived experience in the landscape." Polytheism offered gods and goddesses of mountaintops, of the sea, of childbirth, the sun, rivers, etc., each of them "putting different faces on the divine." Monotheism, on the other hand, "took that all away and removed God from nature." To demonstrate his meaning, Dara leans back and intones, "Our Father, *who art in heaven . . . ,*" his voice emphasizing the latter phrase to suggest that the monotheistic God *art not* in nature.

But Molloy retains an admiration for the early Celtic Christian monks, who, unlike their continental Christian counterparts, "didn't push

6. Molloy, *The Globilization of God*, 322.

7. Molloy, "The Sacred Oak - An Crann Dair."

8. Molloy, "The Sacred Oak."

out polytheism, but put monotheism alongside the old traditions." Celtic Christianity, he writes, "grew organically upon the fertile topsoil of an earlier Celtic spirituality." The three island-goddesses that the "invading Celts" met upon their arrival in Ireland pre-figures the Christian trinity, writes Molloy, and Lugh, the Celtic god of light, is a "Christ figure who defeats the forces of darkness." Even older pre-Celtic Irish spiritual traditions were drawn into the Celtic Christian worldview as well: Newgrange admitting the sun into its dark inner recesses on the winter solstice "prefigures the empty tomb of Jesus, proclaiming light in the darkness, life after death and the resurrection of nature after the severities of winter."[9]

Ultimately Molloy calls himself neither polytheistic nor monotheistic, or perhaps is both/and, and more. Spirituality, he insists, is tied to place, and each individual place "must have its own mythologies, legends, and stories that stitch the lives and culture of the people into the landscape, the climate, and the history of the place where they live."[10] When local spirituality and lore extends over generations, it becomes the "tradition" of the place. But even tradition is subject to evolution and flux, so codifying a spiritual tradition, as is the practice of religion, starves it.[11]

Modern commercial life likewise separates people from the earth, says Dara. He and Tess "try to connect back in every way possible to a sense of place." They grow as much of their own food as possible, linking themselves to the local seasons. They use, when possible, the Gaelic language, which many local islanders still speak. They are building a home using as many traditional materials and methods as possible, reclaiming stones from previous homes built on the location and constructing a thatched roof using grass from the island.

Dara increasingly finds his own spirituality in the landscape, which, he says, "has its own soul, plus the presence of the people who have lived and died on it." Knowing the ancient names of landscape features, as well as the practices long associated with those places, is essential to a spiritual sense of place. A pathway called Jacob's Ladder leads from Dara's house down to St. Ciaran's Holy Well. The name likely dates back to Celtic Christian monastic times, as the Holy Well sits next to the monastic ruins of Ciaran's Church (Tempaill Chiarain). But the well was also probably a sacred pre-Christian site. Visiting this holy well might likely have been part of Druidic

9. Molloy, *The Globalization of God*, 180.

10. Molloy, *The Globalization of God*, 314.

11. Molloy, *The Globalization of God*, 308–309.

practices, honoring the earth goddess Eriu by circling her as the sun god circles her in the sky. "So while the Christian meaning of the holy well has changed, the actual physical practice of circling the holy well has remained the same from pre-Christian times," says Dara.

As a Celtic priest, Dara celebrates the *loca sacra* by offering ceremonies in the Celtic tradition. A wedding service Dara provides might include several Celtic-style blessings. A blessing in the Irish tradition connects the divine feminine of the earth to the divine masculine of the oak. Dara blesses the woman as bride, wife, mother, grandmother; he blesses the man as groom, husband, father, grandfather.

With a blessing of earth, air, fire, and water—since "we on the earth could not live without any of these"—Dara sprinkles the couple with droplets from a bowl of water representing the community. He lights a match above the couple, representing the fire of love and the passion for life. He blesses them with an eagle's feather, representing air, the couple's inner lives. And he taps them with a piece of turf, representing earth and the journeys of their lives.

At the end of the ceremony, Dara blesses the health of the marriage, "a living thing which needs to be nurtured and kept alive." He makes a sign of a Celtic cross upon their hands. ("The Celtic cross precedes Christianity," Dara explains. "Some were found carved on trees by the Druids.") And finally he pronounces a blessing for the protection of their marriage, circling the couple and sprinkling them with holy water.

"Something is awakened in people" through such ceremonies," he says. It connects them back to the landscapes in which they live.

I could have talked with Dara the whole day and more, but after an hour and a half I thought it best to let him get on with his day. I had visited the usual sites in my first trip to Inishmore a few years prior with my wife, so my destination this day was simply back to the ferry pier at Kilronan village. Dara ushered me down Jacob's Ladder to the holy well and pointed me in the direction of the village, but urged me to take a "slow walk" and experience the natural and archaeological sites along the way.

I took his advice and walked deliberately. I circled the holy well seven times and then examined the Celtic cross carved into the standing stone next to the ruins of the monastic church that had stood on the landscape for nine hundred years until destroyed by Cromwell in the seventeenth century. Below the holy well I found the pool that served the monks as drinking water. Its placename, Pool of the Salmon, links the monastery—whose monks probably caught salmon there for eating—to the pre-Christian mythos of the salmon of knowledge and to the Christian mythos of the fish as the symbol of Christ.

I also stopped at the nearby cillín, a graveyard of unbaptized infants. When the conquering Anglo-Normans forced a continental orthodoxy upon the Celtic Christian tradition, its theological victims included those infants who died without baptism shortly after birth. A strict Catholic catechism excluded unbaptized children from heaven and thus from consecrated graveyards. The haphazard scattering of unmarked, rough stones in the hump-shaped hill is a lingering physical manifestation of grief-stricken families—probably quite often mothers alone—burying deceased, unbaptized infants in the middle of the night, filled with equal measures of personal grief and anger at the Church. This teaching and practice of the Catholic Church in Ireland lasted until the 1990s.

The humps of earth and tangle of stones tore at me. I had travelled a quarter of the way across the world, rode a ferry an hour and a half across Galway Bay, sat in Dara's kitchen and shared his bread, and now, instead of returning to Dun Aengus or finding the Black Fort, I stood alone on a hill cemetery of unbaptized infants and pondered the horrors of the past linked to this very ground. Alien to this Thin Place, I could palpably sense but not fully absorb the stories and grief lingered here.

This voyage was further, deeper, and more intense than a tourist visit. This was the place most remote and most austere, my interior self.

THE HOLY INHABITS THE REMOTE, AUSTERE PLACES

To find the "diesart"—the desert—in rain-swept Ireland, do I head for the distant mountains and rock-cropped islands, or retreat within myself? Both, it seems, are pathways to finding the holy in austere, remote places, of finding the Lughnasa sun.

Sailing off to remote physical landscapes was part of the Celtic heart, both Christian and pre-Christian. The Pre-Christian Imrama are a series of voyage tales to the Otherworld and to Tír na nÓg, the land of eternal youth. Perhaps such Irish tales of wanderlust reflected historical waves of migration to the island over land bridge and by sea, dating from Mesolithic times at the edges of the retreating glaciers.

For the Celtic Christian monk, such wanderlust held a specific spiritual goal called "white martyrdom." Red martyrdom was the word for those who gave their lives—their red blood—for the faith, and green martyrdom for those who voluntarily undertook privation. But a white martyr was someone who—individually or in a small community—left behind family, larger monastic communities, places of friendship, of reasonable expectation of sustenance, and set off to unknown destinations for the purpose of interior conversion. White martyrs might embark on rudderless boats without sails, putting themselves at the mercy of the winds and currents and ultimately of their God who may or may not find them a landing place. Surely many perished at sea.

White martyrdom and the quest to "find one's place of resurrection" motivated Aran Island monastic settlements, as well as those in the deeps of the Burren and the bog. Perhaps most iconic among Ireland's outpost monasteries was Skellig Michael, a stark rock of a mountain rising 650 feet out of the Atlantic seven miles off the southwestern coast where sixth-century monks established a monastery for personal penitence. Here a handful of monks lived in stone "beehive" huts, gathered bird eggs and fished for sustenance, worshipped God on an isolated island crag, and died among the rocks. Numerous headstones—shaped by the pounding rain into something more like short, ghostly humans than crosses—rest amid the dwelling huts.

But sometimes the remote, austere place requires not a rudderless voyage beyond the self, but a delving into an even more dangerous interior place, the place of the silent encounter with the self and, perhaps, with one's Maker.

The Celtic Christian hermetic experience symbolically recalled Jesus' forty days in the desert and the tradition of the early Christian desert monks who, beginning in the third century AD, left Rome and other cities of comfort to live in Egyptian desert caves as hermits or in small communities. Noting the requirement of solitude for insight, the Trappist monk Thomas Merton tells of an ancient Egyptian monk in *The Wisdom of the Desert* who went to his abbot seeking advice, "and the elder said to him: Go, sit in your cell, and your cell will teach you everything."[12]

In *The Blue Sapphire of the Mind*, Douglas Christie argues that the experience of an interior desert silence is necessary for developing awareness of the surrounding physical world. Silence, for Christie, is necessary for

12. Merton, *The Wisdom of the Desert*, 30.

"learning how to look, how to pay attention, how to see—learning to avoid missing, through carelessness or inattention, that which is most precious and valuable."[13]

John O'Donohue, in *Anam Cara*, similarly links the practice of solitude to self-awareness: "Only in solitude can you discover a sense of your own beauty. The Divine Artist sent no one here without the depth and light of divine beauty. This beauty is frequently concealed behind the dull facade of routine. Only in your solitude will you come upon your own beauty."[14]

§ § §

I lived alone in Westport, Ireland, for two months. I met wonderful people, hiked with a local hillwalking club, and bicycled with a group as friendly and funny as those I ride with back home. I frequently walked down to Christy's Harvest coffeehouse to write among familiar faces. I skyped Dianne nearly every night. Email kept me connected to my college, and Facebook to my friends and family. And yet I found myself frequently alone for large portions of the day in my apartment or while out for walks. My thoughts flecked out in keyboard taps. I thought of my wife, my grown kids, my friends. While my apartment was neither remote nor austere, this interior silence was undoubtedly so.

Across the Atlantic, back home in North America, we understand the *journey* aspect of wanderlust. The First Peoples arrived by post-glacial migration and then spread throughout the Western Hemisphere. European Americans likewise arrived by mass migration. Today we still get the journey part. We wander for our jobs, we wander to explore new places, and increasingly we wander because we simply want to travel.

It's the interior voyage that we avoid. In my Monastery Voices course, I assign students journal prompts such as going for walks without headphones, driving without their music playing, waking oneself up in the middle of the night—3:30 a.m., the hour of monastic vigils—and listening to the quiet. Initially students are annoyed, bothered, even frightened by the quiet. Some write that they don't like the thoughts that press in upon them in the silence. As the semester rolls along, however, they discover much about themselves in the quiet. Some interior fires have been rekindled.

§ § §

13. Christie, *Blue Sapphire of the Mind*, 141-142.
14. O'Donohue, *Anam Cara*, 103.

The Irish mystic John O'Donohue puts it well: "Ascetic solitude involves silence. And silence is one of the great victims of modern culture."[15]

TREMPEALEAU, WISCONSIN

A slight mist hangs over the Mississippi, and an un-ripened sun has barely cleared the eastern bluffs as I hurry north along the Great River Road. Archaeologist Robert (Ernie) Boszhardt[16] has offered to show me around the Native American mounds at Trempealeau, Wisconsin, and I don't want to be late.

Trempealeau takes its name from the 425-foot rock-mountain island rising from the Mississippi River twenty miles northwest of the city of La Crosse. The island mountain is cut off from the nearby imposing Wisconsin bluffs by the mouth of the Trempealeau River. The name originated with French-Canadian explorers who called the island "la montagne qui trempe à l'eau," the mountain whose foot bathes in water.

Humans have long regarded the bluff-lined river corridor at Trempealeau as both sacred and nurturing. Paleo-Indians hunted mega-fauna beyond the reaches of the glaciers up to twelve thousand years ago, finding refuge from the ice in the Driftless Land. The most prominent remains of ancient Native American culture are the numerous burial and ceremonial mounds on the mountain, in adjacent Perrot State Park, and on the bluffs above the village of Trempealeau.

At first glance, Trempealeau is neither remote nor austere. In the height of summer its river bluffs burst with deep, green forests, and the Mississippi River provides abundantly for fisherman and fowl. Nearby cornfields boast of plenty. Nor is it particularly remote, located just twenty miles from one of Wisconsin's state universities in La Crosse.

But in the eleventh century Driftless, Trempealeau was a distant outpost of the Native American metropolis of Cahokia located nearly five hundred miles downriver. Pleasant and abundant in summer, the Trempealeau

---

15. O'Donohue, *Anam* Cara, 108

16. Robert (Ernie) Boszhardt has focused his career on the archaeology of the Midwestern United States. He worked at the Mississippi Valley Archaeology Center (MVAC) at the University of Wisconsin-La Crosse from its inception in 1982 until January of 2010, holding positions of Staff Archaeologist, Regional Archaeologist, Contracts Director, and Associate Director. He has directed numerous surveys and excavations in the unglaciated Driftless Area and Upper Mississippi River Valley and has published over 50 articles and book chapters on a wide range of regional archaeology topics.

bluffs were stark and the river frozen in winter, especially in contrast to a more moderate climate back home.

Surely the Holy dwelt there.

§ § §

Boszhardt, co-author of the seminal work *Twelve Millennia: the Archaeology of the Upper Mississippi River*, meets me bright, early, and energetically at the visitors center in Perrot State Park. Within moments we are hiking toward the river's edge. With a sweep of his hand, Ernie explains that the park's mounds were built by people who occupied the surrounding area from around 500 BC to 1000 AD during the Woodland Period.

Only a fraction of the mounds and artifacts once located in the park still remain. Many were plundered by amateur and professional archaeologists in the 1800s and early 1900s. In the mid-1960s, the Wisconsin DNR plowed over a number of mounds to create a recreation area. A sandstone shelf that today supports a river overlook appears in an 1880s photograph adorned with ancient petroglyphs. The sandstone was quarried in the early 1900s and the petroglyphs destroyed.

Several burial and ceremonial mounds lie on the island-mountain itself, but many of these, too, have been tampered with. Twenty conical mounds on a bench group show signs of "looter holes," violations dating to the 1800s. Letters from island visitors boasted of men digging up the mounds while the ladies prepared a picnic lunch. Now protected from such abuses, Trempealeau Mountain—steep and pinnacled and accessible only by canoe or kayak—is "peaceful and disturbing at the same time," says Boszhardt, referring to the tampering from the past. [17] One undisturbed bird effigy and linear mound remain higher up on the mountain.

Ernie and I turn away from Trempealeau Mountain and hike south from the visitors center, encountering small remnants of conical mounds, as well as deer and wolf effigies. This was the location of a Woodland period village, Boszhardt explains. For several thousand years, tribes gathered here along the river during spring, summer, and fall, the river offering a plentiful supply of fish and clams with nearby hunting. In winter, villagers dispersed into small bands that took refuge in rock shelters, hunting deer and other game. They over-wintered in the rock shelters, small indentations in the bluffs, protected from the elements by hide-skin or wooden "curtains" strung across the opening. Behind the curtain, the overhanging

17. Boszhardt, Personal Interview.

and back-wall rock retained and re-radiated heat from the campfires. Ernie led me to one such rock shelter where an archaeological expedition had unearthed 2,000-year-old pottery.

For the Woodland peoples, the village at today's Perrot State Park represented the season of plenty, of goodwill, of gathering in the warmer weather and connecting across clans and tribes. But another set of mounds about a mile downstream, located on the river bluffs above the village of Trempealeau, suggest that for another group of Native Americans, Trempealeau was a remote and wintery outpost far from home. Boszhardt and other archaeologists have been actively restoring what may be Trempealeau's most unusual mounds, a set of three large earthwork platforms, the largest rising seven feet above the natural contours of Little Bluff.

Platform mounds such as these are unusual in the Driftless Land, constructed not by the effigy-builders of the Upper Mississippi Valley but by a colonizing group who paddled five hundred miles upriver from the parent city of Cahokia (near present-day East St. Louis, IL) around 1050 AD. Cahokia, the largest Native American metropolis north of Mexico, was a thriving city with an estimated population of up to 40,000 that likewise burst onto the landscape around 1050 AD in what Boszhardt calls the "big bang" of sudden Cahokian formation. Cahokia was the seat of the Mississippian culture that dominated much of the current southern United States but made incursions northward from 700-1550 AD. The city itself lasted until 1300. Archaeologists aren't certain what brought the city down, but it could have involved the environmental impacts of such a large population.

Driving the mile down from Perrot State Park, Ernie and I park on Main Street, which rises precipitously up from the river valley, near the pathway that leads to Little Bluff. Ernie points further up the hill to the farmstead of an early archaeologist whose work laid the foundation for Boszhardt. George Squier had come to Trempealeau as an adolescent in 1864 when his father purchased a farm and was hired as the local Baptist minister. Around 1880, Squier returned east, where he developed an interest in archaeology while studying geology, but ultimately ended up back at the Trempealeau family farm where he soon unearthed from his garden distinctive red-glazed pottery of a style he later linked back to the Mississippian culture.[18]

Not much more happened for a long while to further link Trempealeau to the Cahokian culture. For a while the trail went cold, but archaeological

18. Boszhardt, Email Correspondence.

interest resurfaced by the early 1980s. Digs at that time and in 2010 found much more of this red-glazed Cahokian pottery that the colonists likely had brought along with them from home.[19]

The colonists had hauled with them other life supplies from Cahokia as well. Triangular side-notched arrowheads and knife styles commonly found at Cahokia were unearthed from the village below the mounds. Perhaps not knowing what resources to expect when they settled up north, the Cahokians even brought with them four types of flint stones found only near Cahokia.[20]

Boszhardt points out that footprints of about five Cahokian houses have been found in Trempealeau. Many other structures were undoubtedly destroyed when the town was constructed, so that it is impossible to know for sure how many Cahokians lived here, but all indications suggest it was a small village. Houses were semi-subterranean with wall posts and thatched roofs. Radiocarbon dating indicates that the colony had ended by 1100 AD, having lasted perhaps twenty or thirty years.[21]

But if the village and the colonists' pots, arrowheads, and knives—as well as their earthly bodies—all sank away into the soil in the ensuing centuries, the platform mounds of the Cahokian civilization still crowned the natural landscape, if perhaps a little worse for the wear through the ages.

Platform mounds, as opposed to the conical, linear, or effigy mounds of the Woodland Period, were a signature feature of the Cahokian culture. The platform mounds at Trempealeau and a handful of other Upper Mississippi Valley colonial outposts are smaller replicas of those at Cahokia. Monks Mound at the Cahokia Mounds Illinois State Historic Site rises one hundred feet above the surrounding plane like a two-tiered pyramid with a flat top. Its base measures 970 by 780 feet. Containing 22 million cubic feet of basket-moved earth, the platform was the third-largest man-made structure in the western hemisphere at the beginning of Euro-American exploration. Several smaller platform mounds remain at the Cahokia site as well, and were common throughout the Mississippian culture. The platform tops are thought to have housed both palatial dwellings for community leaders as well as holy temples.[22]

19. Boszhardt, Personal Interview.

20. Boszhardt, Email Correspondence.

21. Boszhardt, Personal Interview.

22. McMillin, *Buried Indians*, 90.

The smaller platform mounds at Trempealeau were initially an enigma for the Trempealeau townspeople when they were rediscovered by archaeologists in the 1980s. These mounds were shaped differently from the more numerous conical, linear, and effigy mounds found throughout the upper Midwest. A water tower had long ago been built atop one of the mounds, leading some villagers to think that that the flat-topped earthen structures on the bluff tops had simply been bulldozed. Trempealeau native and sociologist Laurie Hovell McMillin suggests that potential restoration costs, distrust of archaeologists from the state universities, and a deep-seated denial of the Native American past all likewise contributed to the town's initial skepticism.[23]

The town's attitude about the platform mounds began to change when Ernie Boszhardt, a President of the Wisconsin Archeological Society and an Honorary Fellow with the Anthropology Department at the University of Wisconsin-Madison, began studying Perrot State Park mounds in 1995 and the platform mounds in 2010. Ernie's ongoing immersion in the community and his outgoing personality, as well as generational change within the village itself, opened the villagers to the possibility that their bluffs had housed a colonial outpost of one of North America's greatest early cities.

§ § §

Ernie and I meet Trempealeau resident Ty Webster as we begin our hike up through the woods on a gravel path leading to the platform mounds on Little Bluff. Ty came to Trempealeau in his late twenties several years after his father, like George Squier's, was hired as a local clergyman, and Ty fell in love with the place. He continued living in Trempealeau long after his parents moved elsewhere and retired. Ty wanted to join us because he has also spent considerable time in Ireland, as his brother lives there. Ernie told me that when he explained my project to Ty—Ireland, the Driftless, spirituality of the landscape—Ty said "I'm in!"

Ty explains his attachment to the landscape as we start up the gravel road leading to the bluff: "There are certain places on the planet that hold that unnamable mystique, and Trempealeau Mountain is definitely one of them, surrounded by the fabled waters of the big river, by the little, meandering Trempealeau River and the still, stoic backwaters of the [Trempealeau] wildlife refuge. Water holds its own power." In addition, Ty points to "a stretch of trail that is what I could only term magical. The forest floor is

23. McMillin, *Buried Indians*, 112-118.

covered by ferns, and when it is in full green bloom in the summertime, it has an almost prehistoric feel to it. If it were in Ireland, it would certainly be inhabited by the 'wee people,' and to be perfectly honest, I kind of believe that it is."[24]

Ty makes further connections between Ireland and the Driftless as we continue climbing to the bluff top, such as the mists coming up off the river in the morning and cave openings that lead deep into the earth. Both landscapes offer a "strong energy and resonance of the land that attracted ancient peoples who were more in tune to that than we are" in the present.

I offer what I see as a key *difference*: that in Ireland there has been more or less a continuous lineage and culture since ancient times, resulting in the preservation of ancient sites. Even when local knowledge of the purpose of these sites had vanished, knowledge morphed into lore, turning them into fairy rings and fairy hills. *Something of importance happened here*, lore suggests. Our country, by contrast, has suffered the severance of a cultural link to the land due to indigenous peoples being forcibly displaced by Euro-Americans.

"Disconnect leads to disrespect," adds Ernie.

Near the top of the bluff, Ty and I fade into the background as Ernie resumes his role as tour guide and teacher. As we leave the gravel path and head toward Little Bluff, the first thing we encounter are the "borrow pits" on either side of the walking path, i.e., twenty-foot deep gouges that I first thought were sinkholes but which Ernie explains were the source of soil for the nearby platform mounds. From the borrow pits an estimated 113,000 cubic feet of soil had been excavated by the Cahokians—by the basketful, by hand—to build the mounds.

Finally we emerge at a fresh opening in the forest, just cleared and reseeded earlier in the year. When the mounds were built—and on through the 1800s according to photographs—these bluffs had been prairie, not wooded. With the suppression of prairie fire, the bluffs had forested over.

The three platform mounds descend one by one from the crest of Little Bluff to its tip, about 150 feet; the borrow pits add another 150 feet, so the total length of the complex is about 300 feet—a football field. We are on top of the bluff, with three platform mounds stretching out before us in a descending tier down to the edge of the cliff.

Platform Mound 1 is the highest and largest. Built up and out from the bluff, its sides rise about twenty feet above the natural slope line. In

24. Webster, Personal Interview.

2010-11, Boszhardt and a team of archaeologists dug a T-shaped trench and discovered Cahokian pottery, two fire hearths and the foundation of a building structure between them. Radiocarbon dating of seeds found in the trench matched perfectly with the Cahokian origins for the Trempealeau colony.

Mound 2 is a smaller platform situated slightly below the first, from which a river vista of about 270 degrees would exist if there were no surrounding forest. The solstice and equinox sunrises would be visible from this point. A 2015 trench dig likewise revealed another fire hearth here.

Platform mounds, Boszhardt explains, were not typically used for burials, but were ceremonial temples.

The slope then drops to Mound 3. Here the platform was built by digging *into* the bluff and pushing the soil outward. A dig at this site revealed that the mounds were still used in some fashion by Native American cultures centuries after the Cahokian village had disappeared. It remains a mystery whether the villagers returned to Cahokia, died off, or blended into the neighboring tribes.[25]

§ § §

After an hour or so on the mounds, we drop Ty off at the town library and I take Ernie back to the Perrot State Park visitors center. I have a bit of time before I need to head back home, so I grab a burger and a Spotted Cow at the Trempealeau Hotel Restaurant, and then return to the mounds alone. I need to process what I've taken in. This platform mound structure, this earthscape, both intrigues and eludes me.

I think back to Celtic Irish Lughnasa bonfires celebrating the victory of the sun god Lugh and the early harvest. I think of these plentiful Driftless lands, of clans and tribes coming together in the abundance of summer. Hardly remote, hardly austere.

So I return in winter. And from the comfort of my car travelling sixty miles an hour I can feel the weight of winter grey. The bluffs are deep in snow, criss-crossed by the brown trunks of standing and fallen trees. The river is a scree of ice. When I stop at a roadside overlook, the countryside is silent.

Who would have seen the Cahokian colonists' sacred bonfires lit from atop the platform mounds at Trempealeau? Might word have travelled five

25. An interpretive trail now leads to the platform mounds, opened in 2017. Information available at https://www.tremptrip.com/little-bluff-trail.html

hundred miles back to Cahokia that all was well at the outpost, or perhaps that help was needed? Or were they, like Aran Island monks, simply out there on their own like white martyrs?

But today it's still warm as I climb the path, faster than I normally would with my day coming to an end. With each curve of the upward trail my breathing is heavier, more obvious to myself. My chest heaves, reminding myself of the human package that I am.

The trail upward is a pathway inward as well, and when I arrive at the mounds in the forest clearing I burst into an interior room: the Driftless, the mounds, my body, my self. The Holy in the most remote Thin Place.

THE PORTAL

The morning mist has burned off on this August dawn, and the river is waking up. It looks to be a searing, muggy day as I leave the Julien Dubuque Monument.

Dianne and I are making plans for some late summer ventures before we return to teaching. August is a time for travelling, for avoiding the restlessness of the Dog Days. North, perhaps, where the temperatures are a bit cooler, or to anywhere where there are lakes and streams for cooling off. Across the sea to Ireland, where temperatures rarely rise beyond the 70s.

But another destination on a hot and muggy day is inward where the soul may be as bare as limestone or as crowded and chaotic as a Driftless summer forest.

This interior landscape may be remote and austere, but if sunlight can pierce the clearing and the Holy is encountered there, a wild Lughnasa harvest feast may await the return to terra firma.

Chapter 7

Fall Equinox: Story Gathers in the Landscape

FALL EQUINOX

IT RAINED LAST NIGHT—A hard, though short-lived, downpour accompanied by gusting winds that buffeted the maples and the poplar in my back yard. On this fall equinox morning, leaves half-turned in autumn color lay strewn about the road to the Julien Dubuque Monument like littered pages.

Just before dawn, the eastern sky is speckled with a few residual clouds, low horizontal bars drifting lazily southeast. The sunrise, temporarily obscured, washes the underside of a cumulus cloud in a pink hue. A sharp-edged crescent moon hangs near the rising sun, a writing utensil to etch the morning into the surrounding bedrock.

It is the fall equinox, a day of equal light and dark. In Ireland's Boyne Valley, both the sunrise and sunset light up the inner chamber of the Knowth passage tomb through light tunnels carved into opposing sides of the mound. Here at the Julien Dubuque Monument, when the sun finally clears the eastern cloudbank at 6:48 a.m., it spills past the iron bars into the grave, just as it did on the spring equinox. In spring its message was hope. Now on the fall equinox it reminds us of the two-edged sword of life-giving harvest and death.

We read this landscape like a text, a page half-dark with ink, half-light with unspeakable silence.

THE DOO LOUGH PASS

My first time through the Doo Lough [DOO-Lock, i.e., the Black Lake] Pass was by car, as I was still exploring the winding, poorly-marked roads of western Ireland. The scenery was heavy. An olive-colored bog draped off the twisted cliffs of the Mweelrea [MaWEEL-ree-uh] Mountains, whose peaks were obscured by mist. Patches of scree marked the steepest faces, or corries.

Doo Lough itself, by contrast, was a lovely, clear, cold glacial lake nesting between the mountains. And when I emerged past the southern end of the lake, a sign at the Delphi Lodge announced, innocently enough, "Fresh salmon for sale."

Which was somewhat ironic, given that the Delphi Lodge and the Doo Lough Pass marked the setting of one of the most horrific stories of the Irish Famine.

§ § §

Nineteenth-century Irish rural life was precarious even before the Famine. Absentee British landlords exacted a "pig for the rent" from Irish tenants who tended the landowners' cattle and sheep. In return, Irish families coaxed potatoes from small plots for their own subsistence. The potato was the staple diet for 90 percent of rural Irish tenant farmers.

The land required coaxing. Naturally bog land, certain fields could be converted to small-scale farmland by digging deep drainage furrows and applying a naturally fertilizing mixture of lime, seaweed, and manure to the raised soil mounds between the furrows. Ironically called lazy beds, these potato fields required back-breaking construction.

In 1845 a potato blight swept quickly through the Irish countryside, turning potatoes to mush overnight in the fields. It was followed by another blight in 1846, and several more through the early 1850s. Families who depended on the potato quickly saw their reserves depleted. Many were forced to eat the next year's seed potatoes, temporarily postponing starvation.

But the blight needn't have led to famine. While the potato crop crashed, colonial landlords still exported sheep and cattle from Ireland's fields while by and large prohibiting peasants from hunting or fishing on their estates. Nor were the English disposed to offer relief. Charles Trevelyan, the British Head of the Exchequer, pontificated, "The judgement of God sent the calamity to teach the Irish a lesson. . . . The real evil with which we have to contend is not the physical evil of the Famine, but the moral evil of the selfish, perverse and turbulent character of the people."[1]

So famine it was.

A million Irish died of starvation and another million emigrated in the first years of the famine. Western Ireland—the province of Connacht—was hardest hit with a 28 percent population loss. Heavy emigration continued through the following decades until the population of pre-famine Ireland was nearly halved.

In March of 1849, six hundred starving men, women, and children descended upon a new relief station at the town of Louisburgh in northern Connemara, hoping for food or admission to the nearby Westport workhouse. The officer in command said he could provide neither, and instructed them instead to walk eleven miles south through the Doo Lough Pass to the Delphi Lodge to seek relief.

As night was approaching, the crowd hunkered down to sleep on the streets of Louisburgh, and, according to one account, after a winter storm set in, two hundred lay dead by morning.

The survivors trudged to the Delphi Lodge along sheep paths that wound through the bog.

When they arrived at Delphi the next day, the relief officers couldn't be bothered from their lunch, and told the crowd to wait. Lunch completed, the officers then informed the starving crowd that no food was available, and they should return to Louisburgh. Desperate, some turned to eating grasses from the bog, and died because human stomachs can't digest the food of sheep.

The weather worsened again overnight as the people hunkered down in the Doo Lough Pass. Sleet and heavy winds pummeled the ill-clad, starving people, and two hundred more perished on the second night.

The relief officers from Louisburgh could now feed some of the survivors, as there was work to hire out: the dead needed to be buried. But there were so many dead and so little soil that most were tossed into unmarked mass graves in the glens of the Doo Lough Pass.[2]

§ § §

1. Coogan, *The Famine Plot*, 63-64.
2. MacFarlane, *The Wild Places*, 186-187.

When I returned to Doo Lough a second time, my plan was to walk a portion of the road from Louisburgh to Delphi. I had considered fasting before I walked, but I didn't.

In this second day's light the Mweelrea peaks didn't seem quite so threatening. Sheep on the road, at the side of the road, and off in the bog made the day feel lighter.

I went off the road a couple of times myself, sluicing through the bog in my thoroughly water-proof boots, watching the water squelch away with each step. I wandered down to the pebble-shored lake, clear and slightly tannin-tinted. When I stuck my hand into the water, I found it shockingly cold, and imagined a winter rain pelting down on the physically weakened.

The story of the Doo Lough Pass tragedy soon reached America, whose Irish-American citizens then pressured the British Empire into a more humane response. But the tragedy also resonated with America's Choctaw tribe, who raised funds for Irish Famine relief in 1849, the incident having reminded them of their own Trail of Tears two decades earlier. In 1992, the Irish returned the favor, with a group from Connaght walking the 500-mile Trail of Tears and raising $750 million for world-wide famine relief. Each May since then a fundraising Famine Walk winds its way through the Doo Lough Pass.

The first road through the pass was laid down in 1896, and today it is handsomely black-topped. It is no arduous task to drive through the Doo Lough Pass.

Even so, the tragedy has rooted itself into the sinister landscape. Two memorials mark either end of the Doo Lough Pass, one dedicated to victims of the Irish famine, and one to famine victims everywhere.

The least I could do was to get out of my car and retrace the path.

A handful of cars passed me on the road. A few were parked alongside the road, their drivers observing the monuments. But mostly the road was empty. The bog, on the other hand, was still heaped with the tragedy of 1849. If a foot-long slice of bog turf, or peat, represents five hundred years of compacted semi-decay of reeds and rushes, the Doo Lough incident had only just begun to be subsumed into the landscape.

But an odd observation stuck me after I finished my walk, started my car and drove away. When I was walking, the sheep hooves clattering on the road and the nearby rock outcrops sounded curiously like taps on my keyboard. All those silent faces, munching on bog grasses, tapping, tapping, tapping out a story not their own but somehow written into their bodies.

STORY GATHERS IN THE LANDSCAPE.

The landscape is a text, layered with script ranging from the geologic past to last night's rainstorm. In the North American Driftless, limestone is a Doomsday Book recording the accumulated decaying shells of Ordovician sea creatures layered on sea bottoms 400 million years ago. Metamorphic schist in Ireland's Wicklow Mountains chronicles a continental collision. Drumlin-islands in western Ireland's Clew Bay are littered pages from the scraping glaciers. Two hundred feet of alluvium at the bottom of the Mississippi River footnotes the sediment carried and dropped by glacial meltwater.

Dubuque-born geologist James A. Dockal explains, "To be a true geologist, you have to be able to visualize what once was, you have to be able to interpret, to read the landscape."[3]

The biologist reads another text above the bedrock. My colleague, biology professor Tom Davis, teaching abroad in Dublin, scoops a handful of frog eggs from a Wicklow Mountain bog pond, showing a small group of hillwalkers a gooey alphabet about to burst into a croaking chorus. Each plant explains its immediate location, with mosses in the wettest places, reeds and sedges on slightly drier ground. "Reeds are round and sedges have edges," Tom says, rendering these, too, into the realm of language.

Like a palimpsest of partly erased and written-over script, the human story lies yet above the geological and biological, deepening the text, enriching it, and complicating it. On Achill Island, archaeologist Stuart Rathbone reads the slope of a bog-strewn Slievemore mountain. That slight leveling in the mountain incline and that spotty line of grasses amid the heather, he explains, suggests a subtext, an ancient, buried field wall beneath the bog. A few short hours later we have laid the stony words bare to the sun for the first time in three thousand years.

For the ancient Irish, the landscape was filled with story. Pre-Celtic place names underlie Celtic names which underlie modern names like layers of bedrock beneath a thin soil. The most southerly of the Cliffs of Moher, tapering off in the distance with a sloping forehead and notched nose, is the "Hag's Head," invoking the Celtic goddess Cailleach [CALL-yuck], whose name likely pre-dates Celtic times. an ancient crone with a blue-gray face and a single eye. The Cailleach created the mountains and valleys of the Irish landscape by dropping boulders from her apron, and she tested the

---

3. Dockal, Personal Interview.

mettle of sovereigns who were required to lie with her old bones before assuming kingship. If they did so without repulsion, she would shape-shift into a beautiful young woman and grow old again during their rein, and the land would be fruitful.[4] Honor first my ancient landscape, she seemed to say.

The Celtic tradition of dindshenchas [Din-SHEN-a-haas], or the "poetry of place," told how local places, all the hills and glens, received their names. Nearly two hundred such tales speak of the gods and goddesses who resided here and there and gave their names to places. The Boyne River, or An Bhó Fhinn, mother to Ireland's ancient Neolithic civilization, embodies Bóand, the goddess of the "white cow" who brought wisdom and fertility to the valley. Northern Ireland's hexagonal–columned Giant's Causeway is the work of the giant Fionn mac Cumhaill, who built a bridge to Scotland to steal home the giantess girlfriend of the Scottish giant Benandonner, and then destroyed the bridge to save himself from pursuit. Other versions of the legend likewise explain the oddly shaped Causeway rock structures that arise on either coast and disappear beneath the ocean, not the least of which is the geologists' story of molten basalt erupting from underground pressures and cooling into regular, crystalline columns.

The Celtic mythological cycle continued this tradition of place-naming based on the deeply embedded stories of the landscape. In *The Tain [Toyn]*, the tale of Connaght's Queen Medb's [Maeve's] brash march across Ireland with her minion armies to steal the prized brown bull of Ulster, as well as the brave Ulster warrior Cúchulain's [Coo-HOO-lin's] solo stand against the invaders, nearly every battle ends with a tribute to how the battle place received its name: "Thirty horses fell on that spot, and thirty chariots were smashed there, and the place has been called Belach nAne ever since, the Pass Where They Drove."[5]

The point is not that such places or natural features are named *after* mythological figures, nor that events are simply remembered there, but that the landscape absorbs and embodies the stories that took place upon it like soil absorbing the blood of battle. According to John O'Donohue in *Four Elements*,

> Landscape holds out against transience. While days, years and individuals disappear, it remains. When its surface grasses and leaves die, they fall back into it. It receives the remains of dead

4. Monaghan, *The Encyclopedia of Celtic Mythology and Folklore*, 27.
5. Kinsella, ed. *The Tain*, 92-93.

individuals too; long before it takes their bodies, it has been receiving their lives . . . The earth is ancient memoria. It holds within its layers every happening that ever was.[6]

Even the mundane finds its way into placenames through the landscape of memory. As Noel Dermot O'Donoghue puts it, "Every field, hillock, rock and hollow had its own name. This was the 'meadow of fair grass' and the 'meadow of coarse grass', 'the gap of the horses' and 'the cliff of the cats' . . . [Such names are] fresh and wild and full of the spirit of the hills."[7]

Indeed, the mundane isn't so mundane at all. Although the word derives from the Old French *mondain*, or Late Latin *mundanus*, meaning "of this world, worldly, earthly, secular," for the Irish Celts, the mundane earthly was intertwined with the Divine. Every glen and stream, however plain, had its own local deity. Placenames recorded the intersection of the landscape with the gods and goddesses, the *loca sacra*, the sacred local.

The Celts interpreted the Irish landscape as text in another important way as well. Pre-Christian Celtic literature and lore was oral until the literate early Celtic Christian monks wrote the stories down (possibly layering wisps of Christianity onto the plotlines). But in between the oral and literate Irish cultures came the Ogham [OH-um] alphabet tied inextricably to the landscape. In the centuries prior to Christianization, the Irish traded with the Romans who still occupied next-door England, and perhaps to ease the machinery of trade, the Irish adopted a version of Roman alphabet

6. O'Donohue, *The Four Elements,* 140-141.

7. O'Donoghue, *The Mountain Behind the Mountain,* 4.

called Ogham. Ogham's Roman-based letters were renamed for Ireland's trees and bushes.

The Ogham alphabet of eighteen letters, with some local and period variation, read as follows:

Roman Alphabet Letter	Ogham Marking	Irish Word for Letter	English Word for Letter
A		Ailm	Fir
B		Beithe	Birch
C		Coll	Hazel
D		Dair	Oak
E		Eadhadh	White Poplar
F		Fearn	Alder
G		Gort	Ivy
H		Huath	Hawthorn
I		Iodha	Yew
L		Luis	Rowan
M		Muin	Vine
N		Nuin	Ash
O		Oir	Furze
P		Peith	Soft Birch
R		Ruis	Elder
S		Sail	Willow
T		Teithne	Holly
U		Oir	Heather

While the Ogham alphabet was not widely used by the Irish, some four hundred standing stones with Ogham inscriptions have been found scattered across the island. Most are simple inscriptions of personal names. Even so, this prototype of written Irish language resided in the language of the trees.

The association of story and place did not end with the ancient world. County Antrim native Chris Arthur writes in his essay "Going Home" that emigrant members of his own generation who left behind in disgust the war-torn sectarian landscape of 1970s Northern Ireland were nonetheless unable to experience "belonging" in their new homes across Europe and America because they could not read the landscape. Back home, he says,

> I know precisely at which point on the narrow road that snakes up the hill a favourite uncle proposed to his bride. In a darker register, this is the ditch where a body, hooded and bloody, was dumped, where afterwards, fearfully, we laid flowers; this is where a bullet-riddled car crashed through the hedge and burst into flames . . . Down this road my father drove at breakneck speed one winter's evening forty years ago, bearing my heavily pregnant mother toward my birth . . . The whole landscape speaks when you belong.[8]

§ § §

How long does it take for story to settle in the landscape? Does it soak instantly into the soil like water, or blood? Or does it harden over eons into limestone? Do my stories lie in the Driftless where my ancestors have lived for a surface-thin 140 years? Or am I cut off at both ends, no longer able to read the ancient landscape of my German-Luxembourger forebears and too new to these Mississippi bluffs?

Still, there is nothing to do but move forward. But not having learned this landscape on the laps of a thousand generations, I need an interpreter, a translator, a guide.

I am speaking by phone to Jim Bear Jacobs, pastor to the Church of All Nations in Columbia Heights, Minnesota, and member of the Stockbridge-Munsee Mohican Nation, an American Indian tribe located in central Wisconsin. Jim Bear explains that Native Americans locate the heart of story in the landscape. In the linear thinking of Western thought, he says, time moves in a straight-line fashion, and so Euro-American stories

---

8. Arthur, *Irish Nocturnes,* 238.

exist in time. Locating story in time, however, creates a distance from, and limits access to, stories. "For Natives," he says, "stories are not chronologically linked but connected to places. When we visit the places where certain events occurred, we feel the presence of story in that space."[9]

A Christian minister with degrees in Pastoral Studies and Christian Theology, Jim Bear is the founder of "Healing Minnesota Stories," a program dedicated to interfaith dialog. He considers himself a missionary, "but not in the way most people think." Rather than bringing Christianity to Native Americans, as North American missionaries have traditionally been understood, his goal is to bring elements of Native American ways to Christianity.

His "Healing Minnesota Stories" takes participants to sites intimately tied to Dakota creation narratives and to the intersections of Minnesota history and the Dakota people. "The worst treatment of Native Americans in Minnesota history," he explains, "the U.S.-Dakota war, hangings at Mankato, bounties on Dakota people's heads, and a multitude of deceptive treaties—happens in this brief timeline in 1851-1865. We here in the twenty-first century can distance ourselves from it. But for the Native American mindset, story does not exist in time, but exists in space. Maybe it occurred 150 years ago, but story still exists in this space."

Jim Bear takes his participants into those spaces to "listen to the story. We watch spirits awaken to the stories around them. People understand for the first time that story is 'presence' around them."[10]

Jim Bear told another similar story months later at a conference at Sinsinawa Mound, Wisconsin. In the Twin Cities, Minnesota, where he lives, lies the confluence of the Minnesota and Mississippi Rivers. This, he says, is the center of the Dakota universe, the genesis of their being. Here the Dakota were "created out of materials from the stars and placed on the earth. Every time I descend into that valley I descend into that story of creation." Layered on top of that story, on the very same location, is the story of a concentration camp at Fort Snelling for Native Americans established after the U.S.-Dakota War of 1862. At the beginning of the Civil War, merchants cut off credit to the Dakota in a time of drought, leading to starvation and an uprising by one band of the tribe. After suppressing the insurrection, the Army rounded up *all* nearby Native Americans, not just

---

9. Jacobs, Telephone Interview. And Jim Bear Jacobs and Bob Klanderud, "Awakening to Sacred Space." Podcast.

10. Jacobs. Telephone Interview.

the offending band, and marched the women, children, and elderly to Fort Snelling where five hundred died in five months of overwinter internment.

The confluence of the rivers, says Jim Bear, "holds the stories of genesis and the stories of genocide."

Today, every other year a large group of Dakota women and children, led by a grandmother from the tribe, walks 150 miles in seven days from their reservation to the site, where they commemorate the internment. The children hold a respectful silence, but when the ceremony is over, says Jim Bear, they go off into the woods to play games, explore, and laugh amid the trees, "tapping once again into the song of creation."[11]

I put my burning question to Jim Bear: How deep must ancestral roots be in order to hear the landscape speak? If this aptitude can be lost in a single modern Irish generation of becoming distanced from the land, can the aptitude be gained in a single Driftless lifetime? Jim Bear asserts that there is both a personal and a communal component to hearing the land. First, a person needs to learn the stories of the places we inhabit. "The earth is alive and has identity and spirit that can be accessed if we still ourselves and listen. This can happen individually, but the full flowering takes place in community. When you have a grandmother who carries the stories of place, there's an added depth."[12]

Philip Sheldrake, in *Spaces for the Sacred*, echoes this sentiment that "place" requires the accumulation of memory: "Place is space which has historical meanings, where some things have happened which are now remembered and which provide continuity and identity across generations. Place is space in which important words have been spoken which have established identity, defined vocation and envisioned destiny."[13]

For Sheldrake, "It is appropriate to think of places as texts, layered with meaning. Every place has an excess of meaning beyond what can be seen or understood at any one time."[14]

§ § §

If my ancestors' words and memories are topsoil-thin on this Driftless landscape, I take some inspiration from the Irish peasants of the western islands and the Burren who hastened the process of soil-making by mixing

11. Jacobs, Jim Bear. "Living Stories of Place."

12. Jacobs, Telelphone Interview.

13. Sheldrake, *Spaces for the Sacred*, 7

14. Sheldrake, *Spaces for the Sacred*, 17.

seaweed, sand, and manure. Over time they built up enough soil atop segments of the bare limestone pavements for the potato beds that sustained them.

Maybe it begins by simply listening harder to the landscape.

THE BLACK HAWK TRAIL

The trees were already bare in Dubuque when Dianne and I left for a late-autumn hike at the Black Hawk State Forest in Rock Island, Illinois. But here, just seventy-five miles south of home, the leaves were taking a last valiant hold. You knew it couldn't last.

The Black Hawk Sate Historic Site and Forest occupies 208 acres along the Rock River, only minutes away from the historic location of Saukenuk, the Sauk village that the tribal elder and warrior Black Hawk tried to regain in 1832 for his people after a fraudulent treaty had wrested it from Sauk hands. Today the actual village has long been paved over. A few businesses and an apartment complex in an aging part of town bear Black Hawk's name with no apparent recognition that they sit upon the old village grounds. But in that way they are no different than the innumerable Black Hawk parks, schools, businesses, and even hockey teams that populate the upper Midwest with no real recognition of who Black Hawk was. That said, Rock Island's Black Hawk Historic Site with its 160-acre woods, prairie plot, museum, and bird center pays a slightly relocated tribute to the story of Black Hawk and the Sauk.

Saukenuk in 1832 was no small outpost of nomadic Native Americans. To the contrary, it was a 100-year-old established village of 5,000 Sauk. The Sauk had migrated to the Upper Mississippi from the Great Lakes in the early 1700s. Their new village sat strategically near the confluence of the Rock and the Mississippi Rivers, offering watery highways to the north, south, and east.

Saukenuk was laid out like a modern city, with parallel streets and intersecting alleys, a Council House, and public square. The Sauk lived in "long houses," wooden constructions that sheltered up to fifty people from multiple families. Outside the village, women tended eight hundred acres of corn, pumpkins, squash, and other vegetables. The men fished and hunted. Through the spring, summer, and autumn, the villagers engaged in games and contests, and the young courted and slipped off to the nearby Rock Island to pick berries.

In late fall, the villagers crossed the Mississippi and dispersed by small bands into the Iowa prairie to overwinter, hunting for meat and furs. Each spring they returned to Saukenuk and the cycle repeated.

The Black Hawk State Historic Site museum preserves this story of village life. Nearby, the Black Hawk Forest, one of the least disturbed forests in Illinois with its thick-girthed oak, maple, and hickory hardwoods, preserves the native landscape. Almost thirty-five wildflower varieties bloom in the woods. Birders can catch a glimpse of nearly 175 species, especially in spring migration season. A reconstructed prairie harbors native tallgrasses that tower well above eye-level. In the bluffs above the river once lay 2,000-year-old burial mounds of Hopewellian peoples who predated the Sauk. The mounds are no longer intact. An eighty-foot oak with a five-foot circumference may have actually seen the days of Saukenuk.

A pioneer cemetery on the edge of the grounds is a reminder that Saukenuk would not last. A new bloody chapter was about to begin.

The Sauk had already fallen out of favor with the new American government, having sided with the British in the Revolutionary War and again in the War of 1812. The Americans built Fort Armstrong on Rock Island to keep an eye on things.

In 1804 a group of five Sauk trading in St. Louis signed a treaty which they themselves did not understand and regarding which they had no authority. The treaty, among other things, ceded all land east of the Mississippi—including the village of Saukenuk—to the Americans. Since the treaty would not go into effect until settlers arrived, and since its signatories hadn't understood it anyway, it was not known among the Sauk until they were informed in 1831 not to return to their village the following spring.

Chief Keokuk, grasping the numbers and forces amassed against them, counseled the Sauk for peace and acquiescence. Black Hawk, a prominent warrior of the tribe, disagreed, and with a band of 1,500 men, women, children, and elderly, crossed the river in April 1832 to return to Saukenuk. He'd been led to believe that other tribes would join with him in reclaiming the Sauks' old lands, and that even the British would send supplies from Canada.

When no support materialized, Black Hawk tried to sue for peace, sending a surrender team of five Sauk with a white flag, trailed by another five observers. When Army soldiers spotted the observers, they misread the scene as an ambush and fired upon the Sauk, killing several, including those carrying the surrender flag. A few of the observers escaped to the

Sauk camp, where Black Hawk rallied his warriors for a revenge attack. The Army, as yet undisciplined, fled in confusion and panic, but reassembled with vengeance in mind. The war was on, based on a botched surrender.

It became more of a chase than a war, though. With the Army down-river and regrouping, Black Hawk, with 1500 Sauk in tow, had nowhere to go but upstream along his beloved Rock River, heading northeast, away from the Mississippi. The Army and a recruited militia always trailed a day or two behind.

As the Sauk moved northeastward through Illinois and into Wisconsin, occasional skirmishes blazed across the countryside. Black Hawk and his warriors attacked the Apple River Fort at present-day Elizabeth, IL, where local settlers had taken refuge. A renegade band of Pottawatomie joined the uprising, killing fifteen settlers and taking two teenage girls captive at Indian Creek. But mostly the Sauk were on the run, heading northeast along the Rock River, and they were starving. At Horicon Marsh in east-central Wisconsin, not far from Lake Winnebago, Black Hawk decided to change course and retreat to safety west of the Mississippi. The path, today called the Black Hawk Trail, would make a bee-line across south-central Wisconsin.

The Army first caught up with the Sauk at the Wisconsin River, near today's Sauk City, where Black Hawk and his warriors fought a diversionary battle to give women, children and elderly time to safely cross the river. After the battle, the Army retreated to Ft. Crawford at Prairie du Chien to resupply rather than continue in direct pursuit.

Ill and starving, eating bark from trees and the meat of dying horses, the Sauk pressed through the rugged bluffs and valleys of Driftless southwest Wisconsin en route to the Mississippi. Returning to its pursuit, the Army soon encountered the dead and dying.

§ § §

On an unusually warm late December day, Dianne and I scramble up the steep slopes of Battle Bluff Prairie Natural Area about 35 miles north of Prairie du Chien, Wisconsin, for an afternoon's hike. Owned by the Wisconsin Department of Natural Resources, the bluff rises 480 feet above the valley floor where the final day's battle of the Black Hawk War began. From our vantage point about halfway up the scrabbly, steep-sided goat hill prairie, we are at eye level with surrounding bluff tops. Below, and a half-mile to the west, lay the Mississippi, where the massacre reached full force.

There are no trails here to guide us, so we inch upward by grabbing at the trunks of small trees and, above the forest base, at tufts of grass. The bluff catches the full brunt of the sun. When I slip trying to catch a foothold, my hand lands atop the sun-warmed prairie grass and soil. Above us, turkey vultures circle above, riding the thermals that rise from the baking slopes.

Pausing at an outcrop, we look up the valley, away from the river, in the direction from which the Sauk and their pursuers would have poured.

§ § §

On August 1 the Sauk reached the Mississippi where they encountered the steamboat *The Warrior* that the army had hired out of the nearby town of Prairie du Chien. Again the Sauk tried to surrender, but the steamboat fired upon them at length, killing twenty-three. After a while, the boat returned to Prairie du Chien. The Sauk bunked down for the night along the shore.

If this were a movie, you would raise your eyebrows at the timing. After four months of pursuing the Sauk, always a day or so behind, after battling at the Wisconsin River and then letting the tribe slip away, the Army catches up on the morning of August 2 at the Mississippi shore, halfway between today's Prairie du Chien and La Crosse near the Bad Axe River.

Recording the battle a year later, the *Military and Naval Magazine* reported:

> At length, after descending a bluff, almost perpendicular, we entered a bottom thickly and heavily wooded, covered also with much underbrush and fallen timber, and overgrown with rank weeds and grass; plunged through a bayou of stagnant water, our men as usual holding up their arms and cartridge boxes. A moment after, we heard the yells of the enemy; closed with them, and the action commenced.[15]

Meanwhile, *The Warrior* returned. While Sauk fighters engaged the Army at the shore, soldiers on the steamboat fired away at women with children on their backs and the elderly trying to swim across the Mississippi. The Mississippi River was "tinged with the blood" of Sauk men, women, children, and elderly shot trying to swim to safety across the Mississippi,

---

15. Smith, *Military and Naval Magazine of the United States,*. 16.

wrote Indian Agent Joseph Street, describing the final scene of the Black Hawk War of 1832.[16]

Meanwhile, the Army had recruited the Sioux, enemies of the Sauk, to attack those who scrambled beyond the western shore. Of the 1,500 Sauk who crossed the Mississippi with Black Hawk in April, only 150 survived beyond the August massacre.

Black Hawk himself had left the battle scene in its waning hours, hoping to create a diversion. A few days later he gave himself up. After his surrender, the Army put him on a boat heading down the Mississippi, past Rock Island, not far from his now-destroyed village of Saukenuk. Black Hawk would say in his *Autobiography*, "I surveyed the country that had cost us so much trouble, anxiety, and blood . . . I saw [the whites'] fine houses, rich harvest, and everything desirable around them; and recollected that all this land had been ours."[17]

§ § §

I had intended to explore the Battle Bluff landscape on this last warm weekend of December. But the story of Black Hawk himself has baked itself into the soil and grasses in this Thin Place, and the upwelling thermals still hold the circling raptors aloft like scraps of paper.

THE PORTAL

By the time I'm ready to leave, the ogham letters that blew off the trees last night from oaks nearly as old as the Black Hawk War have now been windswept off the road and onto the forest floor where they'll settle into the soil.

If the stories of the dead have soaked into the landscape, they are humus to the living.

Despite unanswered questions, there is a world I need to attend to, so I get into my car and head back to town.

Light and dark, an equinox, the earth is a text we read but never completely understand.

16. Trask, *Black Hawk: The Battle for the Heart of America* , 286.
17. Black Sparrow Hawk. *Black Hawk: An Autobiography,* 141.

Chapter 8

Samhain: Poets Give Voice
to the Landscape

SAMHAIN, OCTOBER 31

OVER A GUINNESS AND a few long tales at a Dubuque Irish pub, I invite my friend Paul to join me at Samhain [SAH-win] sunrise at the Julien Dubuque Monument. He is, after all, already aware of some of my other eccentric behaviors, like skiing on the golf course under a midwinter midnight's full moon.

Paul accepts the invitation, but since we'll be heading in different directions afterward, we make plans to drive separately and meet at the glow of dawn.

After a warm, colorful October, the month ends in a blustery cold morning of 35° F. When I leave the house, the sky is mostly clear, but an eastern line of clouds threatens to block the sunrise. Here at Julien Dubuque's grave, leaves are dropping with abandon in the stiff northerly wind. Taking refuge on the south side of the monument, out of view of the sidewalk leading down from the parking lot, I'm startled when Paul rounds the tower and appears seemingly from nowhere. As if from a Thin place, I tell him.

We exchange greetings, catch up on news of our grown kids, and cast sidelong glances toward the horizon, where the sun still hides behind the cloud bank. But a few minutes past sunrise, while we're not looking, it emerges more brilliantly than expected . . . and further south, headed toward winter.

We snap a few photos. By accident I capture the sun haloing Paul's head, and, after mentioning this, I snap another shot of him in a deep belly laugh, still haloed. He looks less saintly in this second photo.

With a final toast of coffee mugs, we admit that it's time to head to our respective obligations. But not without offering each other luck for the evening: we both live on one of Dubuque's busiest residential streets, and we each can expect nearly a thousand goblins, witches, and zombies trolling for Halloween candy.

§ § §

The wheel of the year has turned. Samhain marks the beginning, not the end, of the Celtic year, but winter is deeper in the Driftless than in Ireland, and it's hard to see this blustery dawn as the start of something new. Then again, in a circle—or wheel—there is no beginning or end, only a rolling forward in endless cycle.

Be that as it may, Samhain is a liminal time as the year descends into winter, mirroring its six-month equidistant twin, Bealtaine, that bounds into summer. In the Celtic tradition, these were the feasts when the veil between this world and the Otherworld was most likely to dissolve, especially in the Thin Places. The precursor to today's Halloween, Samhain is when "the spirits of the ancestors were venerated," writes Irish Women's Environmental Network founding member Nuala Ahern, and the dead "could communicate with the living."[1]

What stories would they tell?

For if stories settle in the landscape like fallen leaves—or ancestors—then somehow the stories require a calling forth. In ancient Ireland it was the sacred duty of the poets to give voice to the landscape.

KNOCKNAREA

The largest concentration of Neolithic burial sites in Ireland lies just outside the village of Carrowmore, County Sligo, with over sixty tombs dating to 4,000 BC. The burial sites include portal tombs and passage tombs, many of whose cairns have worn away, leaving only their interior dolmen burial chambers and a surrounding circumference of kerbstones.

1. Ahern, "Celtic Holiness and Modern Eco-Warriors," 173-174.

But a wander amid the 900-acre cemetery is haunted by the looming Knocknarea Mountain that dominates the horizon two and a half miles away. From this distance a small rise, known as Medb's [Maeve's] Cairn, is just visible atop the 1,100 foot mountain plateau. The tug on your gaze is magnetic.

An ancient, but lost, story has settled into the landscape at the top of Knocknarea Mountain. No one knows for sure who built the cairn, or why. But so notable a mark on the landscape requires a telling, and so lore is born.

To hear the archaeologists tell it, Medb's Cairn is a 5,000-year-old stone-capped passage tomb thirty feet tall and 180 feet in diameter, the largest of its type in Ireland. The tomb has never been opened or explored in modern times. Nothing is known about who is buried within the dominating structure. Nearby, a dozen other smaller, damaged Neolithic tombs dot the mountain top, aligned north to south and pointing toward Carrowmore. The remains of Neolithic hut sites and debris from stone tool-making have also been found on the mountain top and slopes.

The tomb's historical origins had already been lost by Celtic times, but the bards told a story that wove this landscape into the lore of Ireland. Also known as Medb's grave, the cairn became by legend the resting place of the mythological Queen Medb of pre-Christian Celtic Ireland.

In the epic poem *The Tain*, Medb is a powerful western Ireland goddess-queen of Connacht who convened a morning pillow-talk boasting game with her husband as to which of them had brought the most wealth into their marriage. Since ancient Irish wealth was measured in cattle, the dispute came down to which spouse possessed the best herd of stud bulls. Medb's herd, she discovered to her dismay, was just one bull short of her husband's. In order to secure her superiority, Medb and her legions set out to steal a reputed great brown bull of Cooley from Ulster in northeast Ireland. The famous battles that ensue are recounted in *The Tain*.

Mythology is like bedrock in that there is always an underlying story beneath the one you're trying to tell. In this case, the underlying story is that the men of Ulster, who ought to have been defending their province and riches from Medb's invasion from the west, were incapacitated by a curse put on them by the fairy-goddess Macha, the spouse of an Ulster innkeeper. When a local king held a summer fair, the innkeeper, Crunniuc, made plans to attend, but was warned by Macha (apparently wise to her husband's foibles), "Take care to say nothing foolish." The fair was to include a chariot race featuring the king's horses. When the fair officials boasted, "Nothing is as fast as those horses," Crunniuc, forgetting Macha's warning and the fact that she was at that time pregnant, boasted that his wife, renowned for being fleet of foot, could beat any of the king's horses and chariots in a foot race. The king called Crunniuc on his boast, and ordered the pregnant Macha to run a race with his horses and chariots. He sent a message to her saying Crunniuc "will die if you do not come." [2]

Macha dutifully went to the fair, but pleaded to postpone the race until after she gave birth. The king would not relent, and so she ran the race. Macha defeated the charioteer, but at the finish line she went into labor. Upon birthing twins, she "screamed that any man who heard her would suffer the pains of birth for five days and four nights" [in some accounts, for *nine* months each year], and thus all the men of Ulster and their descendants suffered the annual affliction of labor pains for nine generations. [3]

Many years later, Medb commenced her attack while the men of Ulster were thus incapacitated.

But Medb's timing was foiled because one man, the preeminent Ulster hero Cúchulain [Coo-HOO-lin], was not subject to the curse, not having descended from any man present at the ill-fated fair. Cúchulain was conceived when his mother drank a magical water laced with a worm, and at childbirth his mother vomited him forth. (His virgin birth may have been a detail the Christian monks added to the legend to give Cúchulain Christ-like attributes.) Not afflicted by the curse, Cúchulain singlehandedly staved off Medb's army in daily one-on-one battles, as it would have been dishonorable to send an entire battalion against one man. Each day's battle was immortalized in a dindshenchas [DIN-shen-a-has], a poem telling of how the events of the day led to the place-name of each glen and ford along the battle march.

Cúchulain's strength and heroic prowess eventually wore down, and as he neared death he tied himself upright to a boulder and propped his hands aloft to give the distant enemy the impression he was still ready for battle. He died after three days propped against the stone. Medb's warriors were alerted to Cúchulain's death only after they saw crows pecking at his eyes.

About this time, the remaining men of Ulster recovered from their labor pains and arose to fight the Connacht army. When Ulster finally triumphed over the invaders, even the prized brown bull—the target of

2. Gantz, *Early Irish Myths and Sagas*, 129.

3. Gantz, *Early Irish Myths and Sagas*, 129.

Medb's greed—got into the revenging carnage as it disemboweled and cas-trated Medb's own best white bull.

Medb returned to the west defeated, chastened, and demonized, yet curiously still beloved. The tale of Medb's military prowess may suggest the relative power of women in pre-Christian Ireland. Her demonization, on the other hand, may have been intensified by the early Christian monks who first recorded the story in writing, a cautionary tale against powerful women in a patriarchal order.

The mythological landscape, however, refuses to smear her fame. Also known as Medb's Nipple, the Cairn ensconces her feminine power in the landscape. "Such cairns, common in Ireland, transform mountains into breasts, the earth into a woman's body," says Patricia Monaghan in *The Red-Haired Girl from the Bog*.[4]

§ § §

Leaving Carrowmore, I begin my ascent of Knocknarea Mountain with the goal of reaching Medb's Cairn. A stone path forges upward from Knock-narea Village. The climb is challenging, but not exhausting. After passing through a narrow gate, I lose the path and pick my way up steeper, less defined trails of dirt and stone. For a while, the cairn disappears behind the summit's edge.

As I round the lip of the summit, Medb's Cairn comes into full view, a commanding mound of gleaming white quartzite stones amid the barren, windswept mountaintop. I circle the cairn, taking in Queen Medb's domin-ion. To the east lies Carrowmore, the Neolithic burial site I'd just visited. To the southeast lies Carrowkeel, another Neolithic site. The North Atlantic and Sligo Bay shimmer to the west and north. And to the northeast, Sligo Town, with its holy wells originally associated with Celtic deities and later rededicated to Christian saints.

Winds pummel the mountaintop as I circle the cairn, taking in the prehistoric landscape. I eat a sack lunch among the stones, breaking bread with Medb.

A slight and temporary sun-washed April warmth gives way to chill as clouds roll in, just a breath away here on the summit. With the afternoon waning, it is time to descend the mountain under the watchful eye of one of Ireland's most renowned Celtic goddess-queens.

4. Monaghan, *The Red-Haired Girl from the Bog*, 82.

As a Neolithic passage tomb, the cairn is archaeologically much older than Ireland's Celtic culture that produced Medb's story. But the Celts reframed the tomb as the burial place of their troublesome queen. The Cairn itself is in no hurry to reveal its story. The largest unopened tomb in all of Ireland, the site is now protected, and its mythological tale will remain locked within the rocks.

This mountain, this pile of rock, like many such in Ireland, hints at a mystical past. But here in Medb's fabled land, the poets have given voice to the story in the landscape.

POETS GIVE VOICE TO THE LANDSCAPE

Back in Westport, I wrote in coffeehouses and pubs. Amid the sage-green plaster and dark-stained woodwork of the compartmentalized rooms of McGinn's Pub just one door up from my apartment, I plunked away at my laptop. Sometimes I scribbled in my journal from a barstool while the locals chatted with Antonio, the barkeep.

Down the street at Christy's, I typed out notes and chapters under waves of Americano coffee and slices of apple pie that Christie topped off with cream.

No one thought it the least bit odd to see me writing.

§ § §

Irish Celtic society held poets in high esteem, a tradition that holds true to the present. Occupying a social station just below the druid priests and the Brehon (legal scholars), the poets (or *fili*) of Celtic Ireland were both honored and feared by local kings. A poet, having trained from seven to twelve years in the ways of story and song, might celebrate a good king whose generous spirit had made the earth plentiful. But a miserly king had much to fear from a satirist poet who could expose the king's lack of hospitality and shame his honor.

Poets held magical powers. As Patricia Monaghan puts it, the poet is the ultimate shape-shifter: "In oral cultures, names grant power over the objects named. Because the basic poetic technique— metaphor—names one thing, then changes it to another, a poet could transform the world."[5]

5. Monaghan, *The Red-Haired Girl from the Bog*, 81.

More recent Irish writers have continued this deep connection to place, particularly so in Connacht. Not far from Knocknarea is the burial site of W.B. Yeats, the late nineteenth and early twentieth century poet who strove to pin Ireland's literary and political identity to its magical past. Ninety miles southwest lay the Aran Islands where John Millington Synge captured Ireland's most Gaelic communities in prose and drama. Eighty miles south lay Lady Gregory's estate that nurtured Irish writers and poets and wedded them to the lore and magic of nature during the early twentieth century Irish Literary Revival. The union of writers and nature is captured symbolically on the Gregory estate's Autograph Tree, whose bark is etched with the carved-in names of Ireland's most prominent authors who'd visited the property.

Today's western Irish writers may be less interested in the mythical tradition, but are equally focused on place. Connacht's County Mayo is home to poet and essayist Sean Lysaght, who eschews anything more spiritual than the sighting of birds and eagles thought long extinct. *Irish Times* nature columnist Michael Viney likewise lives in County Mayo, writing unsentimentally about rare plants and animals and the modern threats to their habitat.

§ § §

While the association of poetry with place lore runs deep in Ireland, its roots lie far deeper in the western theological and mythological tradition in which language underlies and precedes the creation like bedrock. "In the beginning was the Word," wrote the Gospel-writer, John, "and the Word was God."[6] In Genesis, spoken words beget the creation. God speaks that there must be light, and there is light. God's first act of naming is "calling the light Day and darkness Night."[7] Theologian David Cloutier explains, "Genesis 1 is best seen as a theological poem, not a scientific account, which depicts the careful work of God in creating all the world through acts of speaking."[8]

In Genesis 2, God then utters the first metaphor, breathing life into soil and naming his human creation "Adam," from Adamas, Hebrew for "soil." In turn, God gives the task of naming the animals to Adam and Eve.

---

6. *Catholic Family Edition of the Holy Bible*, John 1:1.

7. *Catholic Family Edition of the Holy Bible*, Genesis 1:5.

8. Cloutier, *Walking God's Earth*. Liturgical Press, .29.

One needn't be a believer, nor a literalist believer, to understand the power of naming as put forth in the mythological traditions. In an attempt to understand the world—and thus to make it more orderly and more seemingly under the control of higher powers, indigenous mythologies gave names to the powers of nature and assigned these powers to the gods and goddesses. In Celtic Ireland the goddess Sínann's search for the salmon of wisdom led to the naming of the River Shannon. The River Boyne, mother of the cradle of Ireland's Neolithic culture, takes its name from Boand, the goddess of the white cow who brought fertility and plenty to the countryside. At every turn, naming is itself an act of magic, an act of creation.

Among the earth's creatures, humans are particularly adept at language. Other species see better than humans, hear better than humans. Other species taste the air for measure of danger, smell a story out of the ground, and possess enormous powers of grip and thrust. Conversely, humans speak. There is much we still don't know about the communication practices of other species, but there is no doubt that humans make sense of the world through language.

And in speaking sense into the world—breathing meaning into dust, as it were—humans both glorify and continue the work of creation. The Passionist monk Thomas Berry, celebrating the evolution of the universe and its creatures, posits a special role for humans within the universe. "The human," writes Berry, "is by definition that being in whom the universe reflects on and celebrates itself in conscious self-awareness."[9] This does not put humans above other creatures, but it does establish for humans a unique task, at least upon the planet earth. The human role is to sing the earth story, like bird-song.

Jesuit theologian David Toolan describes the human communicative task to be much like the Celtic fili, the poets who sang the graces of deserving masters:

> It is as if the Master of the Universe, the Holy One, had gone out onto the byways and invited us to a glorious feast, the only condition being that in return for the superb food and drink we have and shall receive so abundantly (i.e., all the transformed energy of the sun), we have to tell a wonderful story for our host, the Poet-Maker of the cosmos. It is poet's work, the poet-maker in each one of us.[10]

9. Berry, *The Christian Future and the Fate of the Earth*, 30.
10. Toolan, David, SJ. "The Voice of the Hurricane," 99.

The stones and valleys themselves are silent. The River Shannon itself doesn't tell how it was formed. The cairn on Knocknarea Mountain doesn't reveal whose hands gathered stones and built from them an enormous mound. Landscape may harbor stories like the pages of a book or the screen on your computer holds letter-shapes, but it requires poets to give voice to those stories. Poets probe the silence in the landscape for meaning. Burren poet-philosopher John O'Donohue writes, "Fundamentally, there is the great silence that meets language; all words come out of silence. Words that have a depth, resonance, healing, and challenge to them are words loaded with ascetic silence."[11]

Nature is the repository of stories, but it falls to the poets and writers to imbue the landscape with meaning. Call them geologists and archaeologists, call them theologians and historians, or call them poets, give them musical instruments or give them paint brushes or give them pens and keyboards and the gifts of the storyteller's voice, they—we—re-create the world in terms of human understanding.

§ § §

I wrote in pubs and coffeehouses and in the confines of my Westport apartment. My journal made meaning from what I had seen at Newgrange and along the River Shannon. The act of writing revealed to me what I had only sensed in the moment at Glendalough and in the Burren. Writing in the back room of McGinn's Pub, I returned to the cliffs of County Mayo, and I rediscovered the Cemetery of the Innocents on the Aran Islands. With rain pelting at my apartment window, I finally understood what the tapping of the sheep hooves meant at the Doo Lough Pass. Typing away at Christie's Cofffeehouse, I considered why the Celtic past had hijacked the forgotten story of the Neolithic cairn at the summit of Knocknarea Mountain and named it Medb's Grave.

Then I boarded a plane and returned to America. I wrote from my office at home, I wrote from my back yard. I wrote at the coffee shop down the block from my house. My writing took me back to Ireland. My writing took me back to the Mississippi river bluffs, to the Kickapoo Valley Reserve, to the Trempealeau Mounds, to the Black Hawk Trail, to the Aldo Leopold Shack.

I'm a writer, and yet I don't know how to tell you this: the landscape aches with stories and they must be told. This is all I know to tell.

11. O'Donohue, *Annam Cara*, 119-111.

And so I am on the lookout for a proper poet in my own landscape, one who can read the landscape and give it voice.

THE ALDO LEOPOLD SHACK

The single-storied shack, brown-stained and weathered, sits in the shade beneath pines, aspens, and maples set fifty yards back from the road. A plain white door and a swinging wooden shutter are the only front adornments. A lean-to drifts off to the left.

The shack may not be much to look at, but this weekend-and-summer getaway along the Wisconsin River inspired the pioneering conservationist Aldo Leopold's reading of the landscape in the 1930s and 40s. Along with Henry David Thoreau and John Muir, Aldo Leopold completes the philosophical and literary base of North American environmentalism. His posthumously-published 1949 *A Sand County Almanac* is particularly influential due to its plain-spoken prose depicting a year of seasonal observations from the farm that Leopold and his family nursed back into the wild. The book, Leopold's own dindshenchas, was not a classic until Earth Day in 1970 ushered in the early stages of the modern environmental movement and fueled a new interest in Leopold's work. *A Sand County Almanac* has returned the favor, having introduced new generations to environmentalism ever since then, with over 2.5 million copies sold and published in eleven different languages.

Born in Burlington, Iowa, in 1887, Aldo Leopold developed a love of nature that led him to pursue a career in the Forest Service. First stationed in New Mexico, he initially adopted the conservation credo of the times, namely that eradicating wolves would make for more bountiful big-game hunting. But when he watched the "green fire" fade from the dying eyes of a wolf he'd shot, he slowly began to understand that killing one species to promote another was not only ethically wrong but counter-productive. All life, he would come to realize, was interconnected, and the destruction of any single link endangered the whole.

Leopold's career eventually brought him back home to the Midwest, where he became the nation's first professor of wildlife management at the University of Wisconsin-Madison. Not one to remain for long periods in city life, in 1935 Leopold scouted out a small, abandoned farm property along the Wisconsin River, fifty miles from Madison, for ecological restoration and as a family refuge.

The farm had suffered through the same drought years that created the Dust Bowl further west. Its sandy soil along the Wisconsin River Valley had been depleted by over-farming. Leopold's biographer Curt Meine describes the scene as Leopold first encountered the farm:

> At a forlorn site along the river, there were few pines in sight. Clumps of aspens sprouted along the margin of a frozen marsh. A haggard row of wind-swept elms lined a driveway. The fields, poor and sandy even in the summer, seemed even more barren when gripped by winter. The spent soils supported only sand burrs, their dried heads held out above the snow. The farmhouse at the end of the line of elms had burned down; all that remained of the house was a dug-out foundation. To one side there was a small but sturdy chicken coop, the only structure still standing on the property. They took a look inside the chicken coop and found a year's accumulation of manure piled up against one wall ("When we carry it out and put it under your garden," Aldo later encouraged [his wife] Estella, "you'll be very glad it was there").[12]

Leopold soon bought the property from the County, which had taken possession for back taxes after its abandonment. Much to his wife's and five children's initial dismay, Leopold and his family cleaned up the chicken coop and converted it into the family cabin.

Meine continues his description of the renovated shack:

> The Leopolds and their friends now visited the shack virtually every weekend. They chinked the walls of the shack, and battened them with fugitive planks cast up by the river. Aldo rarely bought lumber; the spring floods always provided. They completed a small side addition to the shack. The shack exterior was plain-unpainted sideboards, a foundation of field-stones, the roof protected by wood shingles and tarpaper. The interior was no fancier—unadorned walls, a clay floor, some shelves and cabinets, a sturdy wooden table, a woodbox, several benches and chairs . . . Cooking was performed in the large hearth, or outside over an open fire. Water came from a pump just outside the door.[13]

Leopold found salvage windows and doors at a junkyard on his walk to and from work in Madison. They used snow fences for bed springs and marsh hay for mattresses.[14]

---

12. Meine, *Aldo Leopold : His Life And Work*, 341.

13. Meine, *Aldo Leopold : His Life And Work*, 375.

14. Kobylecky, Personal Interview.

After converting the chicken coop to a cabin, Leopold and his fam-ily began planting a variety of pines suitable to the sandy soil throughout the property. The first year of pine-planting ran head-on into another year of drought, with failure rates of 90% or more. But the Leopolds persisted, planting over three thousand red, white, and jack pine seedlings every year from 1935-1948. Seventy years later Leopold's pines still grace the sandy-soiled property.

Just north of the shack, a hiking trail through Leopold's pines opens up to the sandy banks of the Wisconsin River. The Leopold Foundation grounds and the "sand counties" that Leopold's book references lie just beyond the edge of the Driftless region, its sandy soils having formed at the bottom of a huge ice-dammed glacial lake 18,000 years ago. Leopold describes its formation in "Marshland Elegy":

> When the glacier came down out of the north, crunching hills and gouging valleys, some adventuring rampart of the ice climbed the Baraboo Hills and fell back into the outlet gorge of the Wisconsin River. The swollen [ice-dammed glacial] waters backed up and formed a lake half as long as the state, bordered on the east by cliffs of ice, and fed by the torrents that fell from melting mountains.[15]

When the ice dam burst, the lake quickly drained, its torrents carv-ing out the downstream Wisconsin Dells before emptying into the Missis-sippi River. The sands left behind as the water level dropped still make the Wisconsin River a sandy anomaly among the Midwest's typically muddy watersheds.

The river's sandy shoreline and shape-shifting islands today are desig-nated an Important Bird Area (IBA) for grassland birds. The Leopold-Pine Island IBA is a mosaic of over 16,000 acres of land owned by public agen-cies, private non-profit organizations like the Aldo Leopold Foundation, and individual landowners. All the partners voluntarily work together to protect critical breeding habitat for over 150 species of birds. Most spec-tacularly, the islands harbor up to 10,000 sandhill cranes during the fall migration season.

Sand and gravel drift formed the upland ridges that today are also part of the hiking trails and prairies of the Leopold Foundation property. The Leopolds re-established prairie by digging up strips of prairie sod remnants as they would find them alongside roadways on their drives from Madison. Aldo transported these back to the shack on the roof of his car and patched

15. Leopold, *A Sand County Almanac*, 97-98.

them into the sandy soil near the shack, from which they spread. This was one of the earliest attempts at prairie restoration.

A stroll through the grounds is best accompanied with a copy of Leopold's epic work, *A Sand County Almanac*. To match the month of my own visit, I open to the *Almanac's* October musings, a month of particularly reflective prose. Here Leopold encounters an abandoned barn, and wonders "how long ago the luckless farmer found out that sand plains were meant to grow solitude, not corn." Still pensive, Leopold observes, "To arrive too early in the marsh is an adventure in pure listening; the ear roams at will among the noises of the night, without let or hindrance from hand or eye." More playful musings note that at daybreak "every rooster is bragging *ad lib*, and every corn shock is pretending to be twice as tall as any corn that ever grew. By sun-up every squirrel is exaggerating some fancied indignity to his person."[16]

Playful or pensive, Leopold gave voice to the landscape.

§ § §

Jennifer Kobylecky, Director of Education at the Aldo Leopold Foundation, swings open the door to the shack and we step inside this simple Thin Place. The humble site burns into my memory. Near the back of the cabin squats a brick and mortar fireplace, its heavy use stained into the sooty mantle. Kerosene lanterns, cast iron skillets, shovels, and hand saws hang from the walls and simple eating ware are stacked on a few built-in pantry shelves. Bunk beds for the Leopold children and a bed for Leopold and his wife are tucked under the sloping lean-to ceiling.

Jennifer and I sit down at Leopold's heavy, thickly-painted dinner table with bench seats tucked neatly into a corner under the swing-out window. Jennifer explains that one of Leopold's motives for purchasing the property in 1935 was to "experiment to see if he could take a property that had been degraded and restore it."[17]

At the same time, says Jennifer, Leopold was acutely aware of the human need to make a living on the land. While he argued for the needs of species beyond humans, he also acknowledged that one of the greatest challenges for the modern world was "to live on the land without spoiling it. He argued for a balance between human needs and the needs of the land community."

16. Leopold, *A Sand County Almanac*, 61-62.
17. Kobylecky. Personal Interview.

At the shack, Leopold kept voluminous records of seasonal data, called phenology, such as when the wild flowers bloomed and the trees leaved, when spring birds returned, and more. Later his daughter Nina moved back to the area and took up keeping phenological records again. In 1999 she published an article noting that spring was arriving about two weeks earlier than in her father's time, and fall was dallying two weeks later on the other side of the year. Nina's was a pre-21st-century voice warning about climate change.

Perhaps Leopold's phenological observations led him to see landscape as a text to be read and interpreted. The theme runs rampant throughout *A Sand County Almanac*:

> The autobiography of an old board is a kind of literature not yet taught on campuses, but any riverbank farm is a library where he who hammers or saws may read at will.[18]

> Now he [the dog] is going to translate for me the olfactory poems that who-knows-what silent creatures have written in the summer night. At the end of each poem sits the author—if we can find him.[19]

> Like people, my animals frequently disclose by their actions what they decline to divulge in words.[20]

> Every farm is a textbook on animal ecology; woodsmanship is the translation of the book."[21]

> Hard years, of course, come to pines as they do to men and these are recorded as shorter thrusts, i.e. shorter spaces between the successive whorls of branches. The spaces, then, are an autobiography that he who walks with trees may read at will.[22]

> In October my pines tell me, by their rubbed-off bark, when the bucks are beginning to 'feel their oats.'[23]

In Leopold's famous February account, "Good Oak," he saws through the annual rings of the trunk of a downed oak and notes the historical events the tree had witnessed throughout its stoic life: "From each year the raker teeth pull little chips of fact, which accumulate in little piles, called

18. Leopold, *A Sand County Almanac,*. 25.

19. Leopold, *A Sand County Almanac*, 43.

20. Leopold, *A Sand County Almanac*, 78.

21. Leopold, *A Sand County Almanac*, 81.

22. Leopold, *A Sand County Almanac*, 83.

23. Leopold, *A Sand County Almanac*, 84.

sawdust by woodsmen and archives by historians."[24] In the essay Leopold's saw cuts quickly through the brief years of his ownership of the land and bites deeper and deeper into the past. The tree rings, exposed to the author by his saw blade, tell of the draining of the Wisconsin marshes in the early 1900s, of the last carrier pigeon killed in 1899 just two counties to the north, of the introduction of barbed wire in the 1870s to section off farm fields, of a youthful John Muir growing up just thirty miles away and sowing the seeds for wildlife preservation.

Leopold carried this notion of reading the landscape into his teaching at the University of Wisconsin-Madison. Leopold told his students: "I am trying to teach you that this alphabet of "natural objects" (soils and rivers, birds and beasts) spells out a story . . . Once you learn to read the land, I have no fear of what you will do to it, or with it."[25]

§ § §

Leopold died in 1948, just after his famous book was accepted for publication. A neighbor's grass fire had gotten out of control, and Aldo went to help rein it in. According to biographer Meine:

> Aldo crossed to the north side of the flames with his [water] pump, evidently planning to wet the unburned grass along the road. As he walked, he was seized by a heart attack. He apparently set down the full pump, lay down on his back, rested his head on a clump of grass, and folded his hands across his chest. The attack did not subside. The fire, still alive but weakened in intensity, swept lightly over his body.[26]

Leopold's children carried on their father's love of nature and treasured his legacy long after his death. In 1982 his widow, sons and daughters established the Aldo Leopold Foundation to promote and support his conservationist ideals. Today additional lands have been added to the original farmstead, totaling six hundred acres of woodland, prairie, and sand river shore.

In 2007 the Leopold Center opened on the approximate site of Leopold's passing as the Foundation's headquarters and a visitors center. The building itself is constructed of matured pines that Leopold and his family

24. Leopold, *A Sand County Almanac*, 16.

25. Meine, *Aldo Leopold : His Life And Work*, 496.

26. Meine, *Aldo Leopold : His Life And Work*. 520.

planted in the 1930s and employs an array of energy-saving technologies to make it the first American building ever awarded zero-carbon-emissions status. The Center tells the life story of Leopold and offers conservation workshops as well as meeting space for environmental and educational groups.

§ § §

The afternoon sun is throwing long shadows across the shack. Jennifer has work to do back at the Center. I want to take a hike through the property before I begin the two-and-a-half hour drive back home. I take a last look around the austere interior as Jennifer pulls the window shutter closed. But Jennifer has a calmness in the present moment about her, and even after she locks the shack's white wooden door, we take a slow stroll to the river bank and back through the woods to the pickup.

Nature and the legacy of Leopold teaches that "there is a different time frame from what I am usually aware of. It teaches me humility," she says. And it teaches patience. Leopold's essay "Thinking Like a Mountain," Jennifer points out, was written years after Leopold had observed the waning of the green fire in the dying wolf's eyes. It took him years to understand the meaning of that moment. It shows us, she says, that "we don't always know what the right answers are" at the moment we have to make decisions.

In the layering of years, Leopold's "emotion recollected in tranquility"[27] had deepened his understanding of the dying green fire.

Jennifer departs and heads back into the Center. I have to decide how long to linger in the warm October sun on this prairie promontory. Just a few miles beyond these glacial-till uplands lies the Driftless Land, and I know it will soon be time to return.

THE PORTAL

My Celtic year above the Mississippi River comes to a close with this Samhain sunrise. But in the Celtic calendar itself, the wheel of the year is beginning a new cycle.

I don't take too literally the claim that spirits move freely between worlds in the Thin Places on Samhain, just as I don't take literally every tenet of my own Christian faith. But I do believe that story is heaped in

27. Wordsworth, "Preface to the *Lyrical Ballad,*." 263.

the landscape and that the poets give it shape, meaning, and voice. From the long-forgotten Neolithic passage tomb atop Knocknarea Mountain the Celtic bards of Ireland constructed the story of Queen Medb. Closer to my home, Aldo Leopold similarly told the story of an abandoned, recovering Wisconsin farmstead.

More importantly, Leopold taught us how to read our own landscapes if we pause for a moment to listen. He taught us how to create our own private dindshenchas.

A gust of wind brings another flutter of leaves to the ground at this Mississippi River bluff. I gather my coffee, my camera, and my stories, and head back to the world.

Conclusion:

A Spiritual Landscape

"THERE IS A SPIRIT alive within the land itself," says Sheila Fitzgerald, a Sinsinawa Dominican sister in southwest Wisconsin.[1] Sinsinawa Mound, located just across the Mississippi River from my home in Dubuque, cradles the motherhouse of about four hundred Sinsinawa Dominicans living and working throughout the U.S. and the world. The name itself is Meskwaki for "the young eagle."

Sinsinawa Mound is one in a series of tall knolls that dot the Driftless horizon every twenty miles or so in a general southwest to northeast line. The domes are remnants of a hard Niagara dolomite limestone bedrock that once sat atop successive layers of shale, sandstone, and older limestone in a slanted plane reaching a thousand miles back to its namesake, Niagara Falls.

Sinsinawa Mound commands the landscape for thirty miles in any direction. Those who are intimate with the area will orient themselves by locating the mound in their line of vision. The Mound will welcome their return from a long trip away.

The line of mounds, sacred to Native Americans, were considered to be stepping stones for the Great Spirit, Manitoumie, as he strode across the Driftless region.

Since 1847 Sinsinawa Mound has been sacred to the Dominican sisters as well, the order having been founded by the Venerable Samuel Mazzuchelli to educate and support Dominican sisters, many of whom became teachers in the then-young or soon-to-be states of Wisconsin, Illinois, and Iowa. As the institution grew, it took to farming to support the sisters in

1. Fitzgerald, Personal Interview.

151

training. For Sheila, her initial attraction to the Sinsinawa Dominicans came through the land. A farm girl herself before joining the order in 1957, she recalls from childhood "walking in the wind and feeling a sense of the spirit alive." Later, at Sinsinawa, "we were surrounded by and within the beauty of the place itself." The Sinsinawa farm contributed to her sense of the sacred, through dairying and processing its own butter. It led to a feeling that "all of this is one, all things are dependent on one another." It was "part of our formation to be in relationship with the land."

Surely this is sacred ground.

§ § §

Sacred ground is not reserved for places of religious significance. Sometimes sacred ground is simply that ground which retains the memory of what has transpired there.

My two-month quest in Western Ireland began on Achill Island. Through channels I don't even quite remember, I connected on my first weekend with Tomás McLoughlin, an Achill mountaineer and historian who was leading a community hike along the Coffin Trail that crested the Minaun Cliffs at the island town of Dookinella. The Coffin Trail was an old funeral path across the mountain used by villagers to carry the dead back to their home parish nearer the mainland. Tall piles of gathered stones still punctuate the trail here and there—cairns on which the coffins could be set while the pall bearers rested.

The next day Tomás walked us through a bog-scape at Doreen, showing us the roofless stone cottage remains of a farming village and the bog patch where he and a buddy were the last to cut turf in their youth. I left a bit of my ankle behind in the bog, or so it seemed as I stepped into a squelching water hole. The audible pop I heard—and felt—was the sound of my ankle finally releasing from the grip of the bog.

A lot had been left behind on this landscape. Cairns on the Coffin Trail and roofless stone cottages. Turf-cuts in the bog. Tomás showed me where to find a local cillín, a burial site for unbaptized infants, on a low mound above the Dookinella Beach. Some simple white stones still marked its presence.

I call this ground sacred, too.

§ § §

So what, then, is a spiritual landscape? Quite often when I use the term, whether in Ireland or in the Driftless, people look at me quizzically and point me to the nearest outdoor shrine or religious grounds. And while I have been moved by many such a place—whether Sinsinawa Mound or a monastic ruins nestled within the Wicklow Mountains—I mean far more than this in calling a landscape spiritual. What I mean is that the world has Thin Places where the tangible and intangible mix.

The following eight principles have guided my thinking about spiritual landscapes—in Ireland, the Driftless, anywhere. They are related to Ireland's Celtic past, although they are not exclusively Celtic. Nonetheless, they give me a new lens through which to view my home:

- The landscape is spiritual: There is more to the earth than its physical nature.

- The Creation is good: The land and its creatures have value of their own.

- The Holy transforms the familiar: Place is enriched and deepened by events that have transpired there.

- Time is cyclical and elastic in the Thin Places: Past, present, and future intermingle when the separating veil dissolves.

- Animals shape the human world: All living creatures share the thin surface of this fragile, blue planet.

- The Holy inhabits the austere, remote places: We need solitude to cultivate an awareness of the earth and ourselves.

- Story gathers in the landscape: Human history and lore settle into the soil like the annual falling of leaves.

- Poets give voice to the landscape: Writers, artists, shamans, geologists, and biologists alike call forth the story from the land.

Just what kind of spirituality am I engaging in here? Judeo-Christian? Indigenous traditions? Non-theistic? I tend to see more similarity than difference among all of these and other spiritual traditions.

A spirituality of landscape invokes awe and wonder, a sense of something both deeper and greater than the physicality of the universe (itself a marvel and a great good thing). Neolithic man marked the solstices and equinoxes for practicality's sake but likely also with something grander in mind—otherwise why not just line up two rocks with the sunrise and call it a day? Pre-Christian Celts—and their indigenous brothers and sisters everywhere—assigned the powers of nature to the gods and goddesses. Judeo-Christian mythology speaks of the mysterious spirit of God "stirring above the waters" as the seven days of Creation begin. The geologist looks at a landscape and wonders what succession of natural forces created it. The common denominator is awe and wonder.

Awe and wonder. Just how was this world—no, this particular river bluff on which I stand—formed? What is the nature of nature? Who among our forebears stood on this same plot of land and perhaps died here, and what does it mean that I can almost feel their story in the rocks and trees and bog? Does it matter if I call all these things "sacred"?

The word "sacred" is etymologically linked to the word "sacrum," the bone at the base of the spinal cord. The sacred arises amid earthy physicality. If we don't also seek the sacred in the earth, we will find only its shadow in the heavens.

§ § §

Two days before I leave western Ireland I am tagging along with the Achill Archaeology Field School as we attempt to unearth part of that ancient layer from the bog.

Field Director Stuart Rathbone is explaining to the students and me why he thinks there may be a 3,000-year-old stone wall buried beneath the bog in which we stand. To the right as we face up the mountainside lies a Neolithic court tomb dating to 3500 BC, its support stones collapsed but its capstone clearly intact. About eighty meters to the left sit the stone foundations of Bronze Age huts, the dwelling places of ordinary folks from 1000 BC. In between, Stuart reads the landscape. A slight leveling of the mountain slope runs in a straight line between the two sites, with the slope resuming below the line. Clumps of grasses amid the prevailing bog mosses likewise run along this line. "Stones beneath the bog can change the chemical composition," Stuart says, creating differences in vegetation.

So we haul our equipment up the mountainside and stake out a rectangle for digging.

If we find something, we'll prove Stuart's hypothesis. If all we find is bog, then Stuart's prediction is false.

We commence digging. The two younger students work uphill from me, struggling to breach the tangled surface of the bog with their shovels.

With a sharp step onto the edge of my shovel, I slice down into the bog. A shovel slicing into the bog has a luscious sound and feel, like biting into an overripe pear. After a few more slices and twists with the shovel, the first wet, matted layer of bog works free, and I carry the black prism to the spoil mat. Then a second matted chunk.

The next slice of my shovel ends in a dull "thunk." Stuart brightens, but realizes it could be a random buried stone. Until he hears the next "thunk," and the next and the next.

The "thunk" is both heard and felt, travelling up the shovel's spine and disseminating through the bog itself. Ears, hands, and feet all register this first strike upon a Bronze-Age stone wall fence buried beneath the Achill Island bog. Each turn of the spade exposes a section of wall to daylight for the first time in three thousand years.

Soon I have unearthed a three-foot section of wall hidden away beneath two feet of bog.

Later, Stuart instructs me to begin cleaning off the buried stone wall, sweeping and removing bits of bog to expose the stonework to the sun. Bog and glittery flakes of schist stone are under my fingernails. Cleaning the site, I scrape my knuckles on stones that have gone untouched for three thousand years.

In one tiny rectangle hidden away on the mountainside, the bog has offered up a small slice of the Achill story, layered upon and swallowed by successive years' growth of bog, and sunning itself for the first time in three thousand years.

Other lives have passed over this ground before, lives replete with tragedy and joy. As for me, I am grinning ear to ear, kneeling in the bog as if it were a sandbox, scraping the years off the stones and nursing them back among the living.

I call this ground sacred.

"There is a spirit alive within the land itself," said Sister Sheila, back home at Sinsinawa. And I have helped to free it here in the bog of Achill Island.

§ § §

This linking of Ireland and the Driftless Region of the Midwestern United States has little to do with a similarity of landscape or climate. It has everything to do with seeing one's home with new eyes. For someone else, it might be Spain's rainswept Galicia that offers a new lens for viewing the plains of Nebraska, or any such places on the globe with which one is intimate. But Ireland and the Driftless are two landscapes I know intimately, and if I can stitch them together to create a spirituality of place, and if you can stitch another two landscapes together, eventually the world becomes a quilt of knitted-together landscapes, each with stories that transform it from a mere location to a place with meaning.

Our threaded stories help maintain the braid of landscape and humanity, the weave of place.

§ § §

I take a final walk along the Great Western Greenway on the morning that I am to leave Westport. A thick fog has erased Croagh Patrick from the horizon. Minus the mountain, the surroundings look a lot like Dubuque.

I am on a train back to Dublin, on a jet back to Chicago, in the embrace of my wife at the end of a bus ride, and the next morning I am at the Julien Dubuque Monument above the Mississippi River in the Driftless Land where the sun, still fresh from Ireland, births past the horizon quite near to Sinsinawa Mound.

And the portal closes.

Bibliography

Ahern, Nuala. "Celtic Holiness and Modern Eco-Warriors." In *Celtic Threads*, edited by Padraigín Clancy, 171-178. Dublin: Veritas Publications, 1999.

Anglada, Eric. "Homecoming." *Wapsipinicon Almanac*, 22 (2016): 28-31.

———. Personal Interview, Dubuque, IA. 22 January 2016.

Arthur, Chris. *Irish Nocturnes*. Aurora, CO: The Davies Group, 1999.

Auge, Thomas, PhD. "Immigration Patterns into Dubuque County up to 1860." Unpublished typescript, Center for Dubuque History, Loras College, Dubuque, Iowa. n.d., n.p.

———. "The Life and Times of Julien Dubuque." *The Palimpsest*, 57 (January/February 1976): 2-13.

Berry, Thomas. *The Christian Future and the Fate of the Earth*. Maryknoll, New York: Orbis, 2009.

Berry, Wendell. "How To Be a Poet." *Given: Poems*. Berkeley, CA: Counterpoint, 2005.

Black Sparrow Hawk. *Black Hawk: An Autobiography*. Original Publication: Cincinnati, 1833. Edited by Donald Jackson. University of Illinois Press, 1987,.

Boszhardt, Robert (Ernie). Email correspondence. 2 July 2017.

———. Personal Interview, Trempealeau, WI. 7 November 2015.

Burbery, Timothy J. "Ecocriticism and Christian Literary Scholarship." *Christianity & Literature*. 61 (Winter 2012): 189-214.

Cannato, Judy. *Radical Amazement: Contemplative Lessons from Black Holes, Supernovas, and Other Wonders of the Universe*. Notre Dame, IN: Sorin, 2005.

Catholic Family Edition of the Holy Bible. New York: John J. Crawley & Co., 1953.

Christie, Douglas E. *The Blue Sapphire of the Mind: Notes for a Contemplative Ecology*. New York: Oxford University Press, 2013.

Clifford, Anne M. "Foundations for a Catholic Ecological Theology of God." In *"And God Saw That It Was Good,"* edited by Drew Christiansen & Walter Grazer, 19-48. Washington, D.C.: United States Catholic Conference, 1996.

Cloutier, David. *Walking God's Earth*. Collegeville, MN: Liturgical Press, 2014.

Coogan, Tim Pat. *The Famine Plot: England's Role in Ireland's Greatest Tragedy*. Macmillan, 2012.

Davies, Oliver, translator and editor. *Celtic Spirituality*. New York: Paulist Press, 1999.

Dockal, James A. Personal Interview, Dubuque, IA. 9 February 2016.

Fahey, Frank. Personal Interview, County Mayo, Ireland. 8 April 2016.

Fitzgerald, Sheila, OP. Personal Interview, Sinsinawa, WI. 28 January 2016.

Flanagan, Bernadette. Personal Interview, Dublin, Ireland. 12 March 2016.

Fremling, Calvin R. *Immortal River: The Upper Mississippi in Ancient and Modern Times.* Madison, WI: University of Wisconsin Press, 2005.

Gantz, Jeffrey, Tr. *Early Irish Myths and Sagas.* Penguin, 1981.

Gibbons, Mary. Telephone Interview. 12 April 2016.

Gibson, Michael. "Dubuque's Irish History." *Julien's Journal*, March 2003: 38.

Heaney, Columban, OSCO. Personal Interview, Mount Melleray Abbey, Ireland. 29 April 2016.

Heaney, Seamus. *Opened Ground: Selected Poems 1966-1996.* New York: Farrar, Straus and Giroux, 1998.

Hoagland, Kathleen, ed. *1000 Years of Irish Poetry.* Old Greenwich, CT: Devin-Adair, 1975.

Indian Country Wisconsin. "Ho-Chunk Treaties and Treaty Rights. http://www.mpm.edu/content/wirp/ICW-105.html. 11 July 2017.

Jacobs, Jim Bear, Telephone Interview. 11 January 2016.

———. "Living Stories of Place." Talk given at "Native Voices: Place and Spirit, Healing and Justice," Sinsinawa Mound, Sinsinawa, WI. 22 October 2016.

Jacobs, Jim Bear and Bob Klanderud. "Awakening to Sacred Space" At Identity, Theology, & Place: Re-inhabiting the Mississippi Watershed, sponsored by the Church of All Nations, 10 October 2015, in Twin Cities, MN). Podcast.

Joyce, P.W., Translator. *Old Celtic Romances.* Dublin: The Educational Co. of Ireland, Limited, 1920. Digitized by Gutenberg Project, 2011.

King, Richard. Personal Interview, Prairie du Chien, WI. 21 September 2015.

Kinsella, Thomas, ed. *The Tain.* New York: Oxford University Press, 2012.

Kirby, Tony. Personal Interview, The Burren, County Clare. 17 April 2016.

Kobylecky, Jennifer. Personal Interview, Aldo Leopold Center. 16 October 2015.

Koch, Kevin. *The Driftless Land: Spirit of Place in the Upper Mississippi Valley.* Cape Girardeau: Southeast Missouri State University Press, 2010.

———. "A Real 'Working' Forest." [Yellow River State Forest]. *The Dubuque Telegraph Herald.* 2 December 2012.

Lake Itasca State Park Information Center. 29 June 2016.

Lane, Beldon C. *Landscapes of the Sacred: Geography and Narrative in American Spirituality.* New York: Paulist Press, 1988.

LeBeau, Albert. Personal Interview, Effigy Mounds National Monument. 28 September 2015.

Leopold, Aldo. *A Sand County Almanac.* New York: Oxford University Press, 1949.

Lowe, Chloris. Personal Interview, La Crosse, WI. 21 January 2016.

Lucey, Ann. "First sea eagle chicks in 100 years take flight in Kerry." *Irish Times.* 5 August 2015.

Lysaght, Seán. "The Eagle and the Precipice." *Dublin Review*, Autumn 2016: 5-15

MacFarlane, Robert. *The Wild Places.* New York: Penguin, 2008.

Mac Nally, Liamy. Personal Interview, Westport, Ireland. 11 April 2016.

Mallam, R. Clark. "Ideology from the Earth: Effigy Mounds in the Midwest." *Archaeology* 35:4 (1982): 60-64.

Marquette, Jacques, SJ. *The Mississippi Voyage of Jolliet and Marquette, 1673.* In *Early Narratives of the Northwest, 1634-1699*, edited by Louise P. Kellogg. New York: Charles Scribner's Sons, 1917.

McMillin, Laurie Hovell. *Buried Indians: Digging Up the Past in a Midwestern Town.* Madison, WI: University of Wisconsin Press, 2006.

Meine, Curt. *Aldo Leopold : His Life And Work*. University of Wisconsin Press, 1988. eBook Collection (EBSCOhost). Web. 23 Dec. 2016.

Melia, J. Craig. "Animals and Birds in Celtic Tradition." Celtic Heritage: Culture, Beliefs, and Traditions of the Celtic Peoples. http://www.celticheritage.co.uk/articles_ animals.cfm. 24 July 2016.

Merton, Thomas. *The Wisdom of the Desert*. Abbey of Gethsemani, 1960.

Millhouse, Phil. Personal Interview, Dubuque, IA. 24 February 2016.

Mitchell, Frank, and Michael Ryan. *Reading the Irish Landscape*. Dublin: TownHouse, 2007.

Molloy, Dara. *The Globalization of God: Celtic Christianity's Nemesis*. Mainistir, Inis Mór: Aisling Publications, 2009.

———. Email Correspondence, 19 June 2017.

———. Personal Interview, Aran Islands, Ireland, 18 April 2016.

———. "The Sacred Oak - An Crann Dair." November 2001. http://www.daramolloy. com/DaraMolloy/Writings/AnCrannDair.html. 11 August 2016.

Monaghan, Patricia. *The Red-Haired Girl from the Bog: The Landscape of Celtic Myth and Spirit*. Novaco, CA: New World Library, 2003.

———. *The Encyclopedia of Celtic Mythology and Folklore*. New York: Facts on File, 2004.

"The Mystery." *1000 Years of Irish Poetry*. Kathleen Hoagland, ed.. Old Greenwich, CT: Devin-Adair Company, 1947.

O'Donohue, John. *Anam Cara: A Book of Celtic Wisdom*. New York: Harper Perennial, 1997.

———. *The Four Elements*. New York: Harmony, 2010.

O'Donoghue, Noel Dermot. *The Mountain Behind the Mountain: Aspects of the Celtic Tradition*. Edinburgh: T & T Clark, 1993.

Ó Duinn, Seán. *Where Three Streams Meet*. Dublin: The Columba Press, 2002.

Old River Shannon Research Group. https://oldrivershannon.com/. 19 June 2016.

O'Leary, Naomi. "Bear Bone Discovery Re-Writes Human History In Ireland." *Phys.Org*. 20 March 2016. https://phys.org/news/2016-03-bone-discovery-re-writes-human-history.html. 1 June 2016.

O'Loughlin, Thomas. *Journeys on the Edges: The Celtic Tradition*. New York: Orbis, 2000.

O'Neill, Sr. Kathleen, OCSO. Personal Interview, Mississippi Abbey, Dubuque, IA. 16 February 2016.

O'Ríordáin, John. *The Music of What Happens*. Dublin: The Columba Press, 1996.

Pope Francis. *Laudato Sí: On Care for our Common Home*. Encyclical, 2015.

"Professor Michael J. O'Kelly." Knowth.com. http://knowth.com/new_grange.htm 7 June 2016.

Rasmussen, Larry. *Earth Community, Earth Ethics*. Maryknoll, NY: Orbis, 1996.

Rodgers, Michael and Marcus Losack. *Glendalough: A Celtic Pilgrimage*. Blackrock, County Dublin: The Columba Press, 2005.

Rule of Saint Benedict. Translated by Boniface Verheyen, OSB. Saint Benedict's Abbey, 1949 edition.

Sellner, Edward C. *Wisdom of the Celtic Saints*. Notre Dame, IN: Ave Maria, 1993.

Shannon Dolphin and Wildlife Foundation. "Shannon Dolphin Survey in Tralee and Brandon Bays." http://www.shannondolphins.ie/. 19 June 2016.

Sheldrake, Phillip. *Spaces for the Sacred*. Baltimore: Johns Hopkins University Press, 2001.

"Site in NE Iowa will become state's first globally important bird area." *The Waterloo-Cedar Falls Courier*. https://wcfcourier.com/news/local/site-in-ne-iowa-will-become-state-s-first-globally/article_4374e625-5895-5679-9893-60ae12f8b0fe.html. 4 May 2014.

Smith, Henry "The Expedition Against the Sauk and Fox Indians, 1832."*Military and Naval Magazine of the United States*. 1 (Aug. 1833). Reprinted 1914.

Stokes, Whitley, ed. *The Tri-Partite Life of Patrick*. Cambridge University Press. Original publication, 1887. Digital Edition, 2012.

Stravers, Jon. Personal interview, McGregor, IA. 21 October 2015.

Toolan, David., SJ. "The Voice of the Hurricane: Cosmology and a Catholic Theology of Nature." In *"And God Saw That It Was Good,"* edited by Drew Christiansen & Walter Grazer, 65-104. Washington, D.C.: United States Catholic Conference, 1996.

Trask, Kerry A. *Black Hawk: The Battle for the Heart of America*. New York: Henry Holt & Co., 2006.

United States Fish & Wildlife Service. "Upper Mississippi River National Wildlife & Fish Refuge." https://www.fws.gov/. 17 June 2016.

Viney, Michael. Email Interview. 24 July 2016.

———. *Wild Mayo*. Castlebar, Ireland: Mayo County Council, 2013.

West, Marcy. Personal Interview, Kickapoo Valley Reserve. 14 October 2015.

Wharf, Jonah, OCSO. Personal Interview, New Melleray Abbey, Dubuque, IA. 28 January 2016.

Webster, Ty. Personal Interview, Trempealeau, WI. 7 November 2015.

Whelan, Delores. "Celtic Spirituality: A Holy Embrace of Spirit and Nature." In *Celtic Threads: Exploring the Wisdom of Our Heritage*, edited by Padraigín Clancey, 13-24. Dublin: Veritas Publications, 1992.

White, Lynn Jr. "The Historical Roots of Our Ecologic Crisis." *Science*. 155 (10 Mar 1967) 1203-1207.

Wilkie, William E. *Dubuque on the Mississippi*. Dubuque, IA: Loras College Press, 1987.

Wordsworth, William. "Preface to the *Lyrical Ballads*." In *Romanticism: An Anthology*, edited by Duncan Wu. Oxford: Blackwell, 1995.

Yellow River State Forest Management Plan. Iowa Department of Natural Resources. January 2009.

Zilka, Placid, OCSO. Personal Interview, New Melleray Abbey, Dubuque, IA. 3 February 2016.

34037725R00098

Made in the USA
San Bernardino, CA
29 April 2019